TEACHING KIDS TO CARE

TEACHING KIDS TO Care

Nuturing Character and Compassion

BETTIE B. YOUNGS, PHD, EDD · JOANNE WOLF, PHD
JOANI WAFER · DAWN LEHMAN, PHD

HR for the evolving human spirit
HAMPTON ROADS
PUBLISHING COMPANY, INC.

Cover design by Jane Hagaman
Cover art © First Light/CORBIS

We would like to acknowledge the following for permission to reprint this material.
(Note: the stories that were penned anonymously, that are public domain, or were previously
unpublished stories written for Bettie B. Youngs, Joanne Wolf, Joani Wafer, or Dawn Lehman
are not included in this listing. Also not included in this listing but credited within the text are
those stories contributed or based upon comments by teens and their parents. Some of the
stories have been modified to better illustrate the points in this book.)

"Kevin" adapted from "Citizen of the Year" by Jennifer L. Youngs from
*Taste Berries for Teens: Inspirational Stories and Encouragement on Life, Love, Friendship
and Tough Issues.* Copyrighted 1999 Bettie B. Youngs. Reprinted with permission.

"Lana" adapted from "Two-Hundred and Fifty-Six" by Lana Bowman from
*Taste Berries for Teens: Inspirational Stories and Encouragement on Life, Love, Friendship
and Tough Issues.* Copyrighted 1999 Bettie B. Youngs. Reprinted with permission.

"Miles" adapted from "His Bracelet" by Steve Hand from
*Taste Berries for Teens: Inspirational Stories and Encouragement on Life, Love, Friendship
and Tough Issues.* Copyrighted 1999 Bettie B. Youngs. Reprinted with permission.

Hampton Roads Publishing Company, Inc.
1125 Stoney Ridge Road
Charlottesville, VA 22902

434-296-2772
fax: 434-296-5096
e-mail: hrpc@hrpub.com
www.hrpub.com

If you are unable to order this book from your local
bookseller, you may order directly from the publisher.
Call 1-800-766-8009, toll-free.

Library of Congress Cataloging-in-Publication Data

Teaching kids to care : nurturing character and compassion / Bettie B. Youngs ... [et al.].
    p. cm.
  Summary: "In Teaching Kids to Care, the award-winning Kids Korps founders present parents with
unique methods and concepts that cultivate caring and compassion in children. By focusing on the
five caring 'Touchstones,' they offer parents ways to surround their children with actions and messages
designed to strengthen character, build self-esteem, and develop inner contentment"--Provided by
publisher.
  Includes bibliographical references and index.
  ISBN 978-1-57174-548-4 (7 x 9 tp : alk. paper)
  1. Moral development. 2. Virtues--Study and teaching. 3. Moral education. 4. Child rearing.
I. Youngs, Bettie B.
  BF723.M54T43 2007
  241'.4--dc22

                              2007024137

                    ISBN 978-1-57174-548-4
                    10 9 8 7 6 5 4 3 2 1
              Printed on acid-free paper in Canada

What Others Are Saying about This Book

Encouraging children to "do unto others" is one of the most significant experiences you, as a parent, can provide. *Teaching Kids to Care* is the parenting book of parenting books in that it demonstrates how helping others gives children increased self-esteem, a feeling of being valued, opportunities to meet different people, useful new skills, and a lifetime of wonderful memories and experiences. When kids learn to serve others, they become empowered, knowing that they can make a difference in the world.

—Jane Seymour, actress, parent

As a sports broadcaster, I know a thing or two about the importance of teamwork. Because of this, I find Kids Korps to be an amazing organization. The authors show kids the value of working together to create a better world, and in the process they become better people themselves. This book, *Teaching Kids to Care,* shows how to implement Kids Korps' winning strategies to make a child a team player in the game of life. With its practical and proven suggestions, this book offers parents a real chance to make a difference in the lives of their children. Kids Korps changed my own kids' lives, and it can change yours, too. Oh, my!

—Dick Enberg, sports broadcaster, CBS Sports

I know firsthand from my clients at Jenny Craig Inc. that the habits we learn in childhood follow us into adulthood. This holds true not only for diet and exercise, but for so many other things, as well. In *Teaching Kids to Care,* we learn there's no better time than the present to instill good habits in our children, especially if we're to raise them to be loving and caring adults. Instilling good values and teaching children the merit in servicing to others will set them on the right path to becoming people who can change the world in the future. I know this because my own kids learned these valuable lessons through Kids Korps, whose founders wrote this book. I highly recommend *Teaching Kids to Care* to all parents who are ready to give their kids a great head start in life!

—Jenny Craig, founder, Jenny Craig Inc.

For more than a decade, Kids Korps has been providing opportunities for children and adolescents to help others in their communities and throughout the world. The results have been more than miraculous. Kids Korps volunteers have demonstrated the core values of empathy, compassion, interdependence, and gratitude and have inspired others to do the same. They have changed the lives of those around them and, most of all, they have developed within themselves the ability to become true leaders and representatives to their peers. This book, *Teaching Kids to Care,* is Kids Korps' gift to parents. It provides proven ideas for real-life methods for raising children to become the leaders and achievers of tomorrow.

—Dr. Keith Kanner, clinical child and adolescent psychoanalyst; host, ***Your Family Matters Show;*** assistant clinical professor of psychiatry, School of Medicine, University of California, San Diego

In my position at Nestlé I have the opportunity to get to know many nonprofit organizations firsthand. I have found none more true to their mission than Kids Korps. For more than a decade, Kids Korps has been lighting the flame of community service in the hearts and minds of thousands of young people. The results have been amazing. More than 18,000 volunteers have participated in more than 5,000 community service projects. The young people that participate in the projects are developing organizational and leadership skills. But more importantly, because of their efforts, communities are being transformed and lives are being changed. The founders of Kids Korps have written this book, *Teaching Kids to Care,* to show parents how they can use their inspired formula to raise children to become positive, compassionate, and responsible. Isn't that what we all want for our children?

—Kenneth W. Bentley, vice president, Community Affairs and Educational Programs, Nestlé USA

Bettie Youngs, Joanne Wolf, Joani Wafer, and Dawn Lehman have done a splendid job in writing a *very important book*. Life is a dash between two numbers on a tombstone . . . we should enjoy our dash and help others enjoy theirs. The values taught in this book are *fundamental* in creating a positive peaceful caring world. A world full of "KIDS WHO CARE" is the world we all want. This book provides the nuts and bolts to help guide parents in lending a hand. Together, we can make the world a *wonderful destination* for future generations. If every parent in the world read this book and acted on the *wisdom of its words,* that would happen.

—Neil Shulman, MD, author and associate producer, **Doc Hollywood** and others; performer, **What's in a Doctor's Bag?** public television; associate professor, Emory University

Teaching Kids to Care offers parents five powerful ways (touchstones) to engage children in opportunities for developing an authentic sense of self, and a genuine caring for the welfare of others. Filled with encouragement and proven techniques learned from the authors' experiences with Kids Korps, this book is an essential guide for every parent trying to raise a child in today's times.

—Michael Popkin, PhD, publisher, Active Parenting Publishers, and author, **Doc Pop's 52 Weeks of Active Parenting: Proven Ways to Build a Healthy and Happy Family**

As a mother of four and a parenting author, I'm always looking for books that have the potential to change the lives of families. *Teaching Kids to Care* is that kind of book. I've seen the difference that community service has made in the lives of my own children. Through their volunteer opportunities, they have developed more compassion for others, higher self-esteem, and a greater willingness to look beyond their own concerns. *Teaching Kids to Care* reinforces what I've discovered with my family—parents can be given the skills and the knowledge to raise children to become inspired leaders and servants for others. This is an important book for anyone who is concerned about the future of our kids.

—Susan M. Heim, author, ***It's Twins! Parent-to-Parent Advice from Infancy Through Adolescence***

As a school administrator, I know firsthand the benefits when young people become involved in activities through which they reach out to help others. The result is more thoughtful, responsible, and leadership-oriented youth. Nothing could be more important to the scholarship of the student—and the well-being of every student in the school—than to encourage them to be of service in their community.

—Michael Teitelman, Headmaster of The Bishop's School

When young people become involved in Kids Korps activities, the results are safer schools and better communities. I firmly believe in the value of providing kids with opportunities to help, support, and assist others—invaluable insight into why we must treat all people with genuine care and concern. Kids Korps experiences encourage children in their development of empathy, kindness, and compassion toward others. When students take these attitudes out into the world and back into their homes, kindhearted, confident young people and happier families are born. This is why what Kids Korps does truly matters.

—Linda Delaney, superintendent,
Ranch Santa Fe School District

Raising a healthy, happy, and capable child is every parent's number-one goal. Teaching children to care about others is one of the surest ways to make this happen. *Teaching Kids to Care* will show you how.

—Linda Fuller, cofounder, Habitat for Humanity
and The Fuller Center for Housing, and coauthor,
Woman to Woman Wisdom: Inspiration for Real Life

Bringing up children who care about others is one of the most important skills parents can impart. *Teaching Kids to Care* gives parents a fresh and comprehensive framework to help them raise children in ways that will not just make them "good kids," but also kids who are "good" for others.

—Jennifer Leigh Youngs, co-author,
**Oh, Baby! 7 Ways a Baby Will Change Your
Life in the First Year; The Moments and Milestones
Pregnancy Journal: A Week-by-Week Companion;**
and the award-winning **Taste Berries for Teens** series

Teaching Kids to Care is an insightful guide for grandparents and others who want to inspire children to get outside themselves and get involved in service and learning about their community. The many ideas this book offers help motivate and teach kids ways of caring in everyday life. What a great way for kids to build long-lasting connections and to learn and grow through experience.

—Tom Endres, vice president,
National Council on Aging, Washington, D.C.

Soul-deep advice, in a skin-deep culture. No society has ever survived its own success, because all before have failed to pass on stewardship and unselfishness to the generations that followed. This empowering book shows us how to be role models worth emulating.

—Denis Waitley, author, **The Seeds of Greatness**

I've learned a lot of life lessons from the extraordinary people I've met through my work as a radio broadcaster. Time and time again, these people have told me of pivotal experiences in their lives that forged the kind of incredible people they became. Those experiences prompted my enthusiasm about this book, *Teaching Kids to Care.* The values and principles espoused have the potential to turn children—including yours—into extraordinary people who truly have an impact on our world and the people in it. We all want to raise children who grow up with a sense of purpose and meaning for their lives. Reading this book is the first step for parents and guardians in making that happen.

—John St. Augustine, radio host on XM Satellite
of **Oprah and Friends,** author, **Living an Uncommon Life:
Essential Lessons from 21 Extraordinary People**

Teaching Kids to Care helps adults *show* their kids how to age well, how to be healthy—spiritually, intellectually, and emotionally. This book provides excellent examples of ways to get our kids on the right path so they can grow to become healthy, caring people.

—David Lindeman, PhD, vice president,
Mather LifeWays Institute on Aging

Teaching Kids to Care is a wonderful book for any person who seeks ways to inspire children to be compassionate, giving, and kind to self and others. It teaches us how to give children lessons in love.

—Rev. Dr. Philip A. Amerson, president,
Garrett Evangelical Theological Seminary

We lovingly dedicate this book to
our families—especially our parents,
our children, and our children's children—
who stand by us in work, in love,
and in learning.

Table of Contents

Foreword, by Larry King   xix

Preface, by Millard Fuller   xxi

Acknowledgments   xxv

Introduction   xxvii

Part 1: "Caring Kids": A Necessity for Today's Times

Chapter 1. Are We Raising Caring and Compassionate Kids?   3

• Is Your Child a Caring Person? • Parenting: The Problem with Doing Too Much—or Too Little—for Our Kids • A Look at Parenting Styles • Moral-Bending Images: How Influential Is the Media on Our Kids? • Good Parenting Is the Key to Raising Kids Who Care

Chapter 2. Why Caring Matters in the Development of Our Children   15

Developing Selfhood
• Why Does Caring Matter? • A Look at the Research on the Importance of Caring • How Kids Korps Helped Us Learn about Kids and Caring

Part 2: Conquering the Obstacles of Healthy Development

Chapter 3. The Five Essential Touchstones   25

An Overview

• Service to Community • Respect for Community • Personal Integrity • Personal Identity • Leadership and Teamwork

Chapter 4. The Touchstone of Interdependence   33

Are We Raising Kids Who Can Depend on Each Other?

• The Touchstone of Interdependence • Kohlberg's Stages of Moral Development • Why Interdependence Is a Good Thing for Your Child: Six Key Benefits • Helping Children "Get" the Lesson: The "Aha Shift" • Four Ways to Instill a Spirit of Interdependence in Your Child • How Robby's Mother Made a Difference • How Interdependent Is Your Child? • Making Interdependent Caring a Part of Everyday Life • Conversation Starters for Parents and Children

Chapter 5. The Touchstone of Connection   51

The Importance of Blending, Bonding, and Belonging

• The Touchstone of Connection • Are Today's Kids on a Shorter Fuse? • Building Strong Connections: Five Key Benefits • Helping Children "Get" the Lesson: The "Aha Shift" • Five Ways to Teach Children How to Connect and Bond with Others • Personality Traits Can Influence How Children Interact with Others • How Miles's and Carlton's Parents Made a Difference • How Socially Adjusted Is Your Child? • Making Connection a Part of Everyday Life • Conversation Starters for Parents and Children

Chapter 6. The Touchstone of Perspective   73

How Does Your Child See His Life and the World around Him?

• The Touchstone of Perspective • Why Perspective Is a Good Thing for Your Child: Six Key Benefits • Helping Children "Get" the Lesson: The "Aha Shift" • Eight Ways to Help Your Children Gain Perspective • How Does Your Child See the World? • Making Perspective a Part of Everyday Life • Conversation Starters for Parents and Children

Chapter 7. The Touchstone of Gratitude   93

Instilling the All-Important "Attitude of Gratitude" in Your Child
• The Touchstone of Gratitude • Why Gratitude Is a Good Thing for Your Child: Six Key Benefits • Helping Children "Get" the Lesson: The "Aha Shift" • Four Ways to Help Children Experience and Express Gratitude • Three Levels of Gratitude • How Kevin's Parents Made a Difference • Is Your Child Living a Thankful Life? • Making Gratitude a Part of Everyday Life • Conversation Starters for Parents and Children

Chapter 8. The Touchstone of Inspiration   111

Helping Children Live Life with Passion!
• The Touchstone of Inspiration • Why Inspiration Is a Good Thing for Your Child: Six Key Benefits • Helping Children "Get" the Lesson: The "Aha Shift" • Five Ways to Instill a Spirit of Inspiration in Your Child • Is Your Child Filled with Inspiration? • Making Inspiration a Part of Everyday Life • Conversation Starters for Parents and Children

Part 3: Making a Difference

Chapter 9. Inspiring Testimonials from Kids Korps USA Experiences   131

• Home Depot . . . and the Casa de Amparo Project • They Really, Truly Believed I Was Santa Claus • Imagine a Room Like This • Carving My Name • Filling Stomachs and Touching Hearts •Bowling with Love • A Boy Named Arturo • Bare Whitewashed Walls • Flowers to Remember • I Wished upon a Shooting Star • Testimonials from Kids Korps Leaders

Chapter 10. Kids Korps USA   153

More Than a Decade of Teaching Kids to Care
• Build It and They Will Come: Kids Korps and Its Vision • Kids Korps: On a Mission • Giving: A Habit of the Heart • Our Incredible Kids • The Value of Kids Korps for Your Child • Volunteerism Is a Family Affair

Chapter 11. Creating a "Caring Epidemic" in Your Community 169

Be the Difference; Make the Difference
• Starting a Movement • Small Changes Make a Big Difference: Ways You Can Better Your Community • Be the Change • Get the Word Out • Gain Support • Know Your Community Leaders

Epilogue 181

Appendix A. Resources for Teaching Kids to Care 183

Appendix B. Suggested Reading 193

Endnotes 201

Index 205

Foreword

Over the years I've been privileged to offer America a front-row seat to nightly conversations with some of the most influential personalities of our time, including presidents, teachers, spiritual leaders, artists, entertainers, heroes, survivors, pioneers, and history makers. I've had a chance to talk with them and ask what makes them tick. One of the things I've learned from them is that being influential is not just about politics and wealth; it's also about heart. Have you noticed that some people are "significant" because they live "in the whole world" and not just their own space? They take into account the welfare of others and don't just focus on themselves. As different as their stories are, what many of them have in common is the making of choices that made a phenomenal difference. They chose to look beyond themselves and reach out to others. They inspire us to look for the best in ourselves, and to do more than merely get through each day.

Yet the growing concern is this: In today's complicated and busy world, is it possible to raise children who will grow up to be the new leaders, history makers, and pioneers? I believe the answer is, "Yes." It's possible, because many parents are willing to help their children develop the character we see in the powerhouses I so often interview.

It may seem that good role models are getting harder to find, but my experience tells me this is not the case. More and more people are choosing to make a difference, and parents have more opportunities than ever to expose their children to this behavior—and model it themselves. Parents need to teach children that doing for others is not only vital, but also an honor. Children will feel better about themselves as they become more aware of the impact they can have on their surroundings.

The need is greater than ever for people not only to care about their family, but also to give of themselves to people in our world community. War has stranded innocent people in refugee camps, where they are cut off from food and medical care and victimized by those who care little for others. Closer to home, shocking stories unfold in homes, schools, and neighborhoods—brazen violence, callous brutality, and extreme poverty of the spirit.

Therefore, it's important to strengthen the moral fiber of our country—starting with how we raise children. If we want to ensure a brighter tomorrow, there's no better place to start than in our own home and in our own community. What a great opportunity we have to raise our kids to care! When unselfish parents model good character and teach the importance of caring for others, they raise children who will be influential in positive and productive ways.

Magic happens when children see beyond their needs and learn from real heroes. This book coaches us on the importance of parenting and shows us how to raise "kids who care," by building a deep sense of character and compassion in children and society. The concepts in this book can have a dramatic impact on children who will go on to influence the world around them. The world can *always* use more leaders, heroes, and pioneers—and this book can help you help your child be one of them.

—Larry King, *Larry King Live*

Preface

Caring for others is a fundamental basis for good character. The Bible and other religious literature teach us that loving our neighbors is equally as important as loving ourselves. Experience tells us the same thing. Anytime we lend a hand to others—be it through personal gestures, volunteerism, or community service—our hearts are uplifted. The traits of caring and altruism are certainly ones we wish to see in our children—knowing they are qualities that will allow them to become adults who can and will make a difference in their families' lives and in the world around them.

Children learn by example and, as parents, we are their first and most effective teachers. Our actions and our words set the blueprint for their characters. Through our examples, we must instill the fundamental precept of altruism in them at an early age. To neglect the teaching of caring and altruism is likely to lead our children to a naturally human instinct of selfishness. We live in a society where youngsters are bombarded by advertisements, news broadcasts, entertainment stories, and TV programs that so often seem to foster a culture of "me-ism" and greed. If we do nothing to counteract those influences, our children will grow up as self-absorbed individuals, with no awareness or concern for needs or situations beyond their own narrow self-interest. Society sorely needs individuals whose values have been shaped to give them a personal and world view of themselves as loving, caring, engaged persons who want to leave the world a better place than they found it.

When we nurture our children in caring and giving to those in need, they begin to see and understand how even small gestures can have an enormous impact—not just on a personal level, but on a greater social scale as well. Furthermore, such a mindset, formed in childhood, will impact attitudes and actions when our children become adults—the future leaders of our society.

As a parent, and the founder of Habitat for Humanity, I have had the wonderful opportunity to see how even small gestures—both at home and in the community at large—can create a world of difference. My wife, Linda, and I always tried to instill a spirit of caring and giving in our four children. We would do this both by verbal teaching and by example. Our children, for instance, from very early ages, were actively involved in our work of building houses for those in need, both in the United States and in many of the some 100 countries where we introduced our housing ministry. From their earliest years, our children were able to see the concrete results of their caring actions toward others, and have seen how that example has been passed down to our grandchildren. My youngest daughter, Georgia, encouraged her two daughters, Sophie and Jasmine, to give money to The Fuller Center to help victims of 2005's devastating Hurricane Katrina. The girls sent their few dollars, and I sent each child a receipt accompanied by a cover letter expressing thanks for their generosity and the ways in which their contributions would go to help others. The girls were ecstatic, not only because they received letters of appreciation, but also because they learned how their efforts had truly helped the condition of another human being. The wonderful feeling engendered by knowing she had made a difference prompted our older granddaughter, Sophie, to create and sell a gift basket, which provided her with even more money to help the hurricane victims. I sent her another letter of appreciation. When she received that letter, she told her mother, "I'm going to save it in my drawer. I'll take the letter out and read it when I'm sad!"

Even through small, yet significant, gestures parents can daily reinforce to their children the importance of altruism. Not only will those youths understand how they are helping others in need, but they also learn that giving makes them feel good as well. When the children get a chance to turn their passion into action, they will discover that their efforts really *mean* something—to others, and to the future of our world. As a result, they will become capable, confident, and caring citizens—people who really make a difference.

This book, so well written and presented, is a powerful impetus to encourage parents and other child caregivers everywhere to make sure that the teaching of caring and altruism is deeply imbedded in the hearts of every child under their influence. I encourage you to read these pages and recommit yourself to teaching these lessons to your children. When you do, you can help expand the cycle of caring and work toward creating a better world.

—Millard Fuller, founder, Habitat for Humanity,
founder and president, The Fuller Center for Housing

Acknowledgments

We are especially thankful to our agent, Bill Gladstone, and the talented staff at Hampton Roads Publishing Company—especially Jack Jennings, Tania Seymour, and Jane Hagaman—for believing in our message and in us. It has been our pleasure to work with you. Thank you to Susan Heim, Elisabeth Rinaldni, Shirl Thomas, and her assistant Sandy Chené for their sensitivity in the course of editing this manuscript.

We'd also like to express appreciation to the many parents and their children who were an important part of this work. We would especially like to share a heartfelt thank-you to those who gift us with their love and loyalty, and support us in all the ways we choose to step into and fulfill our own destinies. Certainly, that list for each of us is boundless:

From Bettie: To my parents, five siblings, and many cherished friends for their love and inspiration. Above all, for the splendor of a soul-deep relationship with my precious daughter, Jennifer, and her Steve and baby "Kendahl-Bears," who on a daily basis remind me of the real joy of boundless love and caring.

From Joanne: To my husband, David, for his love, encouragement, and daily support; my children: Collin, Lindsey, Julia, and Matt, whose generosity of spirit in action has been my delight and my inspiration; my mom and dad for their example of love and caring; Sharon Wong for her technical support; and my treasured friends, for their constant humor, encouragement, wisdom, and kindheartedness. I am especially grateful for the support of Peggy Callahan, Ellen Stiefler, and Jean Hamerslag.

From Joani: To my loving husband, Chuck, who has patiently supported me throughout the years; my children—Debbie, Steve, Nicole, Jarred, Christina, and Patrick—who have been my inspiration and perfect examples of kids who care; my mom and dad who taught me the true meaning of giving and love; all my wonderful grandchildren, siblings, and friends; and to our dedicated Kids Korps staff and volunteers for their commitment to our mission, "to instill in today's youth the spirit of giving through volunteerism."

From Dawn: To my inspiration and love, Charlie, my constant cheerleader; my children: Steve and Kyle who have given me purpose and joy, Scott and Matt who really know how to care about others, and Mark who shows unconditional love; to my daughter-in-law, Karen, who is a great mom; my grandchildren: Robert, Michael, and Matthew who are growing up to be awesome, loving kids; my mom and dad, who taught me the meaning of kindness and compassion; my siblings and in-laws who live a life of love; my dear friends whose wisdom I will never forget; and our incredible Kids Korps volunteers. I love you all with all my heart!

And from each of us to each other: We are thankful for the opportunity to engage in what has been a demanding and enriching exploration into a collective wisdom of our life experiences. And as always, we give thanks to God, from whom all blessings flow.

Introduction

Every parent strives to raise a healthy child. Teaching children to care, not only about themselves, but also about others, is one of the surest ways to help kids maintain good health through being happy and well adjusted. Our children are the joy of our lives and the hope for our future—two great reasons to teach them how to balance their own needs with the needs of those around them. In this regard, we parents can use some help in guiding our children.

How can we encourage our children to develop caring hearts? They're probably not going to learn this from their friends, and don't count on a TV documentary on the subject anytime soon. Nor is teaching values up to the schools, although more schools are requiring that students engage in community service and character education. It's really up to *you* to inspire your children to genuinely care about others.

Teaching Kids to Care gives parents a fresh and comprehensive framework that helps them raise children to be not only "good kids," but also kids who are "good" to others. This book goes right to the heart of our concerns today: engaging kids in positive behaviors and activities that will decrease boredom, feelings of alienation, self-centeredness, and violence—to name a few. Using this book as a resource will help you to see the untapped potential in your children and prepare them to become tomorrow's informed and compassionate adult citizens.

We are our children's most influential teachers. When parents or guardians help their children practice the five touchstones we talk about in this book—interdependence, connection, perspective, gratitude, and inspiration—they aid in building strong character and nurture young spirits. In short, our children will learn to care about others.

Through our work with Kids Korps USA—a nonprofit youth volunteer organization—we have researched, experimented with, observed, and documented the benefits of teaching kids to care. Now we want to share what we have learned with others who have the will and desire to help children grow emotionally, intellectually, and spiritually. The temptations of today's world can make the job of parenting tougher than ever, but we believe we've found a plan for raising kids who can rise above these challenges to become productive, caring, and happy individuals.

In chapter 1, the process of *teaching kids to care,* we question parenting styles that reflect two extremes in parenting: lack of involvement to overindulgence. Leaving youngsters alone to fend for themselves often results in producing self-absorbed children who never learn to think beyond their own needs. But on the other end of the spectrum, the overinvolved parents not only push their children to excel, but tend to step in and do the work for them—which also encourages self-absorption.

Chapter 2 covers research that concludes: Kids who assist, support, and look out for the good of others are happier and more productive, and experience greater physiological and psychological benefits than those who are centered on self. Moreover, caring about others helps to balance tendencies which, if left unchecked, give rise to selfishness, self-absorption, and bullying.

Chapter 3 offers a brief overview of our five "touchstones" for helping kids learn to care about themselves and others.

The spirit of interdependence, highlighted in chapter 4, teaches children to be there for others—to help, support, and assist in times when it's necessary and, additionally, feel comfortable in asking for help if and when they need it. Children working with and for others develop a moral code and can help resolve some of the concerns that parents and society have about today's children.

The bonding experience we address in chapter 5 is about helping our children establish deep, rich, and rewarding relationships. Children who bond with others gain a sense of belonging, experience the feeling of being appreciated, and grow in their ability to be empathic toward one another.

Chapter 6 explains how kids who have the ability to see things with expanded vision, or through others' eyes, are more compassionate. They're less likely to bully and belittle other children who are "different" from themselves and will be more likely to respond to the needs of others and to prioritize their own needs and desires in balanced and healthy ways.

Chapter 7 emphasizes the importance of instilling the "attitude of gratitude" in our children and stresses their need to discover and understand how cultivating a grateful attitude can bring much joy to their lives. We discuss the five ways to help children experience the heart-expanding effects of gratitude.

Chapter 8 asks the question: How do we create a child who is inspired and who inspires others? We examine how to jump-start a lackluster child, and how to help retain motivation in a wonderful, kindhearted child.

In chapter 9, we share inspiring testimonies that truly demonstrate the life-changing effects of teaching kids to care. These testimonies, from children, parents, and others who have witnessed firsthand the powerful impact of community service and volunteerism, verify that children who help others become more competent, develop strong character, and acquire a huge capacity for compassion.

The story of Kids Korps unfolds in chapter 10. Our vision has not changed over the past twelve years: to broaden kids' perspective on life, helping them to connect with others in special ways. Depending on one another inspires children to take positive action and, above all, influences their having grateful hearts. This can make them leaders for life!

Finally, chapter 11 offers ways to start a movement of compassion and emphasizes how small changes *can* make a big difference.

So how do we mobilize our children to use this compassion to strengthen the communities in which we live? As parents and citizens, we have the power to create a positive family environment for our children and to inspire them to be catalysts of change.

Throughout this book, we show how the five touchstones are interrelated. We believe: The more our kids combine interdependence, connection, perspective, gratitude, and inspiration in their daily lives, the more likely they will be happy, healthy, and productive. And that's what it's all about . . . what we dreamed for them since the day of their birth.

Teaching your children to care is the greatest gift you will ever give to them. Through your guidance and efforts, they will grow into competent, compassionate adults with admirable characters— the kind of people who naturally draw others to them, simply by being in their presence. Yes, you have the ability to make this kind of difference in your children's lives and, in so doing, you—and your children—can also make the world a better place. It is with great hope and heart that this book will serve you to that end.

—The authors: Bettie, Joanne, Joani, and Dawn

"The world sorely needs the healing influence of a great surge of simple thoughtfulness and kindhearted-ness. Such a surge is beyond the power of the world's greatest rulers or statesmen. It must start with us, as individuals. Right in our home communities we average citizens can establish the spirit and set the pattern of a kindlier world."

—Robert R. Updegraff

PART I

"Caring Kids": A Necessity for Today's Times

Removing ice plants from
a nature preserve

A five-year-old volunteer gets into
the action of removing graffiti in
an inner-city neighborhood.

Twin brothers cleaning up after sorting
canned goods at a local food bank

Kids of all ages come together to
assemble disaster preparedness
kits for Hurricane Katrina victims.

1
Are We Raising Caring and Compassionate Kids?

"Doing a good turn may seem a trivial thing for us grown-ups, but a good turn done as a child will grow into service for the community when she grows up."

—Lady Baden-Powell Olave

By all accounts, Eddie was a good kid—considerate, good-natured, responsible, and genuinely concerned about the needs of other people. His mother described him as "a fun-loving boy with a great sense of humor who simply loved being with others." Everyone seemed to agree with her assessment of him as a "people person." On the soccer team, the coach lauded Eddie's natural talent but lamented his lack of competitive edge. It seems Eddie would chat up with everyone—even the visitors on the field, asking, "Where do you live? Is it as humid there as it is here?"

Eddie's problem, the coach said, was his focusing more on people than on winning.

And yet, on November 11, 1994—in a quiet, middle-class neighborhood in Philadelphia—an unthinkable event happened to that sixteen-year-old boy who loved people.

A group of kids from a suburb across town sought revenge. Someone had spilled a Coke on the lap of a girl from their crowd.

They chased down a bunch of kids and caught Eddie, who, when the chaos hit, had stayed in the danger field to help his girlfriend and his little brother to safety. They beat him with baseball bats, holding up his body to kick and punch him further before a full audience—twenty-four kids in all. Five teenage boys brutally beat Eddie, while the other boys and girls watched without intervening. Although the authorities rushed him to the hospital, Eddie died several hours later.[1]

It's difficult to imagine such a horror, isn't it?

Nothing excuses the lapse of character in these kids, nor their indifference at the sight of others pummeling a young man right before their eyes. Certainly, anyone can become paralyzed by fear and uncertainty but, at such times, internal resources can pull us through. If any of those kids had commanded the murderers to stop, had rallied the others to step forward to save Eddie, or restrained the bat-wielding boys, it might have saved Eddie's life.

The kids in the crowd easily outnumbered the attackers, so why hadn't they helped Eddie? What went wrong?

Is Your Child a Caring Person?

Thankfully, our children will most likely not face such dire circumstances. All the same, seemingly, many of today's youth do not value human life in the way we would hope. Once, on a national radio show, the host asked the listening audience, "If a stranger and your pet were drowning, whom would you save first?" Eighty-two percent of all teens who called in said, "I'd save my pet," adding, "because I don't know the stranger." Jaw-dropping aside, as important as it is to know what moral code failed these young people, it is just as crucial for parents to ask, *"How, exactly, would my own child[ren] have reacted in this situation?"*

As for what happened to Eddie, it's not enough to know that your child wouldn't have joined the bat-wielding kids who literally beat the life out of him. But, would your child have stood and watched, doing nothing to stop his murder? Or would your child have rallied to get others to help save this boy's life or gone for help? These tough questions require parents not only to speculate about what their children would do, but also to know for sure if their children would have the consciousness to care about others.

Take a moment now to consider how your child would respond in the Eddie situation—or even at the sight of anyone bullying a child. Would he/she:

- yell at the attackers to stop?

- encourage others to overpower the attackers?

- go for help?

- want to help but would wait for direction from those around him/her?

- wait for the others to do something first?

- run away from the scene at the first hint of any altercation?

- be too traumatized and afraid to intervene?

- try to beat off the attackers by him/herself?

Knowing your child's likely behavior in this situation can help you assess his or her capacity for caring and compassion. The sad reality comes in our awareness that scenes like Eddie's are not isolated events.

Are we teaching our children how to react with kindness?

We parents need not feel baffled about how to raise kids who will look out for the welfare of others. Yes, it requires diligence but, even in today's times, when it seems as though so much is out of control, we can instill the value of caring.

Our kids need role models. And to be a good model, we need to know what moral code we hope for our children. Could it be that the children who witnessed Eddie's beating didn't grasp what they were seeing? When these kids were called as witnesses, police showed concern about the many kids who watched Eddie's beating and lied about what they witnessed, or "couldn't remember" exactly what they saw.[2] What can cause this kind of disconnect?

When kids lack empathy for others, their behavior can range from simply inconsiderate to the unthinkable. Helping your child to develop the skills of compassion and caring for others can lead to better self-leadership and good overall character.

"Kids who assist, support, and look out for the good of others are happier, more productive, and experience greater physiological benefits than those who do not; but the even greater benefit is that caring about others helps to balance tendencies which, if left unchecked, give rise to darker sides of human nature."

—Michael Popkin, PhD, author, *Doc Pop's 52 Weeks of Active Parenting*

Parenting: The Problem with Doing Too Much—or Too Little—for Our Kids

Parents have a lot of influence in their children's lives. Kids may rebel or complain, but they do listen to what we say and watch what we do. As parents, we are our children's first and most important teachers. How we parent matters. Every conscientious parent strives to incorporate the best and most effective parenting actions that will result in raising competent, compassionate kids with good character.

A Look at Parenting Styles

Parenting is complex, and no simple strategies exist. "Parenting style" refers to the broad overall pattern of parental actions and attitudes, rather than to a single act. The following descriptions of four styles of parenting grew out of the work of Diana Baumrind's[3] initial three, and also from other results of researchers in child development. These four styles of parenting come from two important parameters: responsiveness with warmth and support, and behavioral control.

Authoritarian parents attempt to shape, control, and evaluate the behavior and attitudes of the child, in accordance with a set standard of conduct. They dictate how their children should behave, stressing obedience to authority and discouraging discussion. They demand and direct, expecting obedience, and do not encourage give-and-take. They have low levels of sensitivity and do not allow their children to disagree with their decisions.

Authoritative parents set limits and rely on natural consequences for children to learn from making their own mistakes. This type of parenting focuses on teaching the importance of rules and why the children must follow them. These parents reason with their children and consider each child's point of view. They set high standards for future behavior, while encouraging the children's independence.

Permissive parents may be accepting and warm, but exert little control. They set few and inconsistent limits, do not impose rules, and allow children to set many of their own. These parents allow considerable self-regulation in regard to schedules and activities, and tend to avoid confrontation. They do not demand the high level of adherence to certain behavior that moderately authoritarian or authoritative parents do.

Uninvolved parents demand even less and respond minimally. In extreme cases, this parenting style might constitute neglect and/or rejection.

Understanding your particular parenting style—the things you say and do that form the basis for your children's behavior—is not only important but imperative.

Parenting techniques can range from hands-off parenting to over-involved parenting. Neither extreme is optimal for our kids, and both can lead them to a lack of caring about others. Leaving children to fend for themselves with little parental control and involvement (hands-off parenting) often results in self-absorbed children, or children who, without guidance, become more susceptible to peer pressure or influences outside the family.

At the other end of this spectrum are over-involved parents who have earned the title "helicopter parents" because they constantly hover over their children, not allowing them to mature through their own experiences. Such parents not only push their children to excel, but they frequently do the work for them. In all fairness, and noteworthy, these parents have flourished in the incubator of the competitive world that has absorbed our youth. They want to protect their children from failing, but can damage them by doing their work for them and, in essence, by fighting their battles. If Johnny procrastinated on his project or could use a little "assistance" to get a better grade, his over-involved parents would probably complete the project for him. They have good intentions; after all, Johnny's project means a grade, the grade goes on a transcript, and the transcript must hold merit if Johnny wants to get into college—and a good one, at that. But the overall results are dire for Johnny. In this scenario, he learns that someone else will always do his work, and he has no conception of the inevitable consequences because of his lack of involvement. Instead, he learns that when he makes poor choices, someone will invariably bail him out. Not only do kids like Johnny become less capable, but they also become more selfish and self-absorbed, and less likely to develop the skills of working with others for a common good.

Another kind of dangerous hands-on parenting grows from overindulgence. This smothering type of behavior comes through when parents cater to their children's every desire and deprive them of nothing. These parents often suffer from deprivation themselves, missing out on their own wants and needs in order to provide their children with a "better life." They're afraid their children may have to experience the consequences of their actions and, therefore, want to first soften the blow. They must get over it; otherwise the children grow up believing they are the center of the universe and that "it's all about me." Self-centered, they come to believe, "I'm better than you, and so I don't have to help you"—and they don't.

Although we want to protect our children, in order for kids to go confidently into the world, they must know—from the inside out—they can count on themselves and be counted on by others. They need caring parents to help them grow, and they need the confidence to fend for themselves. Children who proceed through life accumulating internal fortitude have the makings for successful adulthood and a life of meaning.

Volunteers are inspired to read to young Head Start preschoolers.

Moral-Bending Images:
How Influential Is the Media on Our Kids?

Without a doubt, we have entered an age of technology with no precedent. Today's children have many advantages. Information and exposure to the world around them lie literally at their fingertips through computer technology; and broad television programming provides more opportunities for learning than ever before. But how much television and computer time do your kids engage in each day, and at what consequence? If you're like most parents, you have to take a moment and think about it. Statistics reveal that one child out of ten comes home to an empty house. These kids, more than likely, will choose passive entertainment. And, not only home-alone kids, but many children have succumbed to an electronic world. According to a recent study, the average child spends nearly 6.5 hours a day with electronic media—television, video games, computers, and music venues.[4]

Does it matter?

We've always blamed television to a certain degree for exerting a negative influence on our young—and for good reason. Although all television programming isn't a vast wasteland, experts tell us that too much television viewing is not good for children. A couch potato often suffers with childhood obesity, which contributes to poor health. And research confirms that the quick sound bites meant to keep viewers' attention negate a productive, developing brain. (The evidence convinced the American Academy of Pediatrics to issue the recommendation that children under two should refrain from watching television altogether.) In spite of the negative findings, parents may still use the TV as a babysitter. The average preschool child spends more than two hours a day in front of a screen.[5] And kids who spend hours in front of a television will, of course, spend less time outdoors or reading.

Numerous studies show that viewing violence can lead to more aggressive behavior, desensitization to violence, or antisocial behavior in our children.[6]

Television is not, of course, the only "screen" that delivers moral-bending images to children. The computer has a hand in it, also. A husband and wife were all ears one day when their eight-year-old daughter came to them saying she couldn't get the "naked people" off her computer. Alarmed, her parents instantly went to the child's screen—lo and behold: a pornography site! When they tried to back off the site, they kept getting more and more pornography, until they finally had to exit the Internet completely. As it turned out, their sweet young girl had accidentally misspelled Disney, leading her to the porn site. They shared their tale with friends, who told them about the many pornography sites deliberately set up to use misspelled names that appeal to children's interests in an attempt to lure them to their sites.

In 1961, social psychologist Albert Bandura conducted a now classic experiment called the Bobo Doll study. Dr. Bandura's research measured aggression in children.[7] The youngsters were put into two groups—one group was exposed to nonaggressive behavior and the other, aggressive. The first group observed a model playing peacefully; the second witnessed the beating up of and yelling at a plastic Bobo doll. Then, they purposefully frustrated the children by withholding toys, before taking them to another room to play. Children who witnessed aggression were significantly more likely to imitate hostile behavior. When Bandura and colleagues studied children viewing aggression toward the Bobo doll on television, they reported similar results.[8]

Of course, not all children who watch too much TV or stumble across a porn site on their computer will readily pick up a bat and beat the breath out of other children.

Despite the sometimes less-than-ideal role models the media

can have on our children, parents can have the power to influence their children more than they know.

Children learn through observation—of family, the media, and the environment. Parents must question, "what actions do we model?"

In the opening (true) story about Eddie, most of the teens did not wield bats, but they didn't seek to help Eddie, either. So while we, as parents, strive to do everything in our power to prevent our children from aggressive behavior, we must also do everything in our power to ensure they are not too dispassionate in protecting and caring for others. A child who spends too much time in passive isolation— glued to the TV set or the computer screen—becomes self-absorbed, and self-absorption diminishes a child's ability to recognize the needs of others. A child who doesn't see the need in others won't help others, and a child who won't help others often looks out for his own needs at the expense of others—which is what we saw mirrored in the kids who didn't mobilize and come to the aid of sixteen-year-old Eddie. Certainly, this is not what we wish for our children.

> "Until the great mass of the people shall be filled with the sense of responsibility for each other's welfare, social justice can never be attained."
>
> —Helen Keller

Good Parenting Is the Key to Raising Kids Who Care

Think again about Eddie and the kids who stood by, witnessing a brutal beating. The child-witnesses certainly outnumbered the attackers. Why did none of them think to harness the power of the group—to work as a team—to intervene on Eddie's behalf? Some might say they didn't interfere because they feared for themselves, but why didn't it occur to them that they could act together? We always hope that such caring about others is instinctual but, more likely, it is a product of parents and other positive influences teaching children to look out for, and protect, one another.

Luckily, it's never too late to begin to teach your children how to react and interact humanely. Michael Josephson, founder of the Character Counts Coalition and Josephson Institute of Ethics, laments about the "hole in the moral ozone" of our youth today. According to a survey by the Josephson Institute, 60 percent of teens surveyed (more than 36,000 high school students) said they have cheated on exams; more than one in four admitted to stealing from a store; and 82 percent said they have lied to a parent about something important.[9]

We can teach our kids to have a sound character, but it does not happen overnight. Building good character in our kids may take hard work; however, it's imperative to help them learn to step outside themselves and care about others. When we rear kids who care about each other, who are concerned about the problems in their community and show *compassion* for others, they develop good *character*. When they start thinking beyond their own small slice of the world, they become *competent* adults who can make a difference. Building competence in our kids empowers them to act, and competent kids will more likely take charge of their own lives and be less swayed by others. We can strengthen the moral fiber of our kids to better make good decisions and feel confident in taking charge of caring for others.

2
Why Caring Matters in the Development of Our Children

Developing Selfhood

"The most important thing in any relationship
is not what you get but what you give . . .
In any case, the giving of love is an education in itself."

—Eleanor Roosevelt

For a great many of us, one of the most inspiring events of our lives is to give birth to or witness the birth of our children. Even before they're born, we caress the rounded tummy of the mother-to-be with anticipation and love. We have dreams—great dreams—for our children and want them to be happy, healthy, and productive. We envision ourselves being the best parents in the world. After the first wave of excitement subsides, and our young toddlers have learned to say "no" and "mine," we quickly realize the challenges of parenting and can use all the help we can get. That's why Dr. Spock—and those who followed—had great success in providing advice to parents.

Reality surely hits when our "perfect" child first bites, strikes, or grabs the toy of another child. *Uh-oh,* we realize, *we have some work to do!* We want to raise "good" kids, who are considerate of others, generous, polite, and well behaved. We want to raise curious kids who want to engage themselves in learning all about the world around them—even in the throes of all their growing pains. They will have awesome winner days along with days when life teaches them that skinned knees and heartaches are just part of learning, growing, and changing; we want them to learn to roll with the punches.

During their early years, we still sit back and smile at the miracle of it all; then comes school and, along with it, new friends, television, video games, iPods, and the Internet. A whole new world opens up to them . . . and we realize the real challenge has just begun. All of a sudden, we're no longer the only influence in their lives, and that's a bit unsettling. With the whole constellation of issues our children face—drugs and alcohol, bullying, intense competition, the threat of terrorism and youth violence—we know in our hearts, the best defense comes in teaching our kids about competence and compassion, and helping them grow up with good character.

Why Does Caring Matter?

Wouldn't it be great if raising a wonderful child were simply a matter of following an easy, foolproof recipe: Three parts kindness, hugs, and kisses; two parts firm boundaries; one part safe communities and good schools—and voilà!, a happy, healthy, and confident child.

While every conscientious parent has general ideas about how best to parent, the truth is, there is no simple recipe—many factors influence our children's health, happiness, and well-being.

Over the years, and especially in our work with young volunteers, we have come to learn the essential ingredients in helping children learn to act and react with kindness—which we find can be cultivated by teaching them interdependence, connection, perspective, gratitude, and inspiration. Caring, giving, and getting outside of oneself are mandatory actions we must use in developing the next generation of leaders—leaders who will make our communities better places in which to live. Someone once said that a good message is both timeless and timely. Teaching kids to care is timeless in that through the ages we have been told of the blessings that come from living a life of caring. Teaching kids to care is also a timely message for twenty-first century parents as they look to find a way to help raise happy, balanced children.

Raising caring kids benefits both our communities and our kids' development.

A Look at the Research on the Importance of Caring

Researchers David McClelland and Carol Kirshnit designed a study that measured the effects of kindness on the human immune system. In their research, subjects watched different films. Those subjects who saw a film of Mother Teresa caring for people in Calcutta had a sharp rise in their salivary immunoglobulin A, which indicates a positive immune system response.[1] In other words, simply watching someone giving to others can strengthen our physical resilience.

Sonja Lyubormirsky, a leading research scientist who studies happiness, has this to say about its benefits: "A recent review of all the available literature has revealed that happiness does indeed have numerous positive byproducts, which appear to benefit not only individuals, but families, communities, and society at large. The benefits of happiness include higher income and superior work outcomes (e.g., greater productivity and higher quality of work), larger social rewards (e.g., more satisfying and longer marriages, more friends, stronger social support, and richer social interactions), more activity, energy and flow, and better physical health (e.g., a bolstered immune system, lowered stress levels, and less pain), and even longer life. The literature, my colleagues and I have found, also suggests that happy individuals are more creative, helpful, charitable, and self-confident, have better self-control, and show greater self-regulatory and coping abilities."[2]

Certainly, today's agendas can lead to more stress-filled times for parents and children. But evidence shows that caring about others can lower the stress in our lives. Hans Selye's now-classic book *The Stress of Life* (1956) maintains that prolonged stress damages our health. In his book, he proposes a way of life to counter the negative effects of stress. He termed this way of living "altruistic egoism" and defined it as "the creation of feelings of accomplishment and security [in ourselves] through the inspiration in others of love, goodwill, and gratitude for what we have done or are likely to do in the future."[3] In other words, we help ourselves when we help others. Selye, who brought the word *stress* to the scientific vocabulary, was convinced: Each of us wants to feel needed and useful in our lives, and our health benefits when we do.

Also noteworthy: The research of Lisa Berkman and Leonard Syme found that variables such as social support, integration, social networks, social participation, and self-esteem are closely related to health. In a study of nearly 7,000 people over a nine-year period, they found those who lacked social and community ties were more than twice as likely to die during the study period than those who had more social relationships. This seemed to be true regardless of race, income, level of activity, and other lifestyle factors.[4]

Author Dawn Lehman and other researchers at the University of North Carolina at Greensboro designed a program to help youth with and without disabilities become actively involved in their communities through volunteering. Over an eight-month period, three groups of youth participated in the program. A total of twelve youths with disabilities (ages ten to seventeen), thirty-eight youths without disabilities (ages ten to seventeen), and two junior leaders (ages nineteen and twenty) participated. The youths with disabilities had mild to moderate mental retardation, mild to severe developmental delays, traumatic brain injury, sensory impairments, and cerebral palsy.

During weekly sessions, the kids participated in team-building activities. They learned about volunteerism (i.e., individual benefits of volunteering, its importance to the community, how to become involved in volunteer activities) and then completed a volunteer activity—which included building and filling flower boxes for Habitat for Humanity families, making pencil boxes for nursing home residents, and planting a patriotic flower garden. Program data were collected through pre- and post-participation audiotaped interviews and through observation. Results of the program included increased understanding of volunteerism, social interaction, belief in self, and sense of responsibility.

Teen mentoring new volunteers while planting a flower garden

Working together to plant trees

**Developing friendships
with Special Olympics athletes**

Early on in the program, several of the youths, both with and without disabilities, expressed fear with regard to becoming friends with strangers from visibly different backgrounds. The volunteers without disabilities were "scared" that they would not do or say the right things. By the program's conclusion, communication flowed between the two groups as they began to establish their own language. They addressed each other by name, laughed together, held hands, hugged, worked together, and took pictures of each other. One program participant said, "In the beginning I was shy, but now that I'm used to seeing them (peers with disabilities) and being around them I'm used to it now. It's just like being with a regular friend." The group leaders observed that many of the participants' belief in self had been greatly impacted when they discovered they not only could interact with their peers with disabilities, but were also good at it. The majority of youths without disabilities stated how they enjoyed the inclusive environment and would choose to volunteer in groups that included youths with and without disabilities in the future.[5]

How Kids Korps Helped Us
Learn about Kids and Caring

In 1994, we started Kids Korps USA, an organization that teaches children the value of serving others and their community. For the past several years, we have dedicated ourselves to understanding what empowers kids who care about others and the world around them. As Kids Korps has grown through the years, we have observed a difference in kids who give to others. Many seem to be cultivating strong positive qualities such as competence, confidence, and responsibility and, with these qualities, a strength of character.

Through our own volunteer experiences, we know how getting outside of self can lift one's spirit, make life more worthwhile, and cultivate internal joy. We have all reveled in the "soul hits" that come from giving. And now we have the wonderful opportunity to watch this happen, as children engage in the numerous activities that encourage them to think of more than themselves.

Kids Korps provides opportunities for thousands of young people—ages five to eighteen—to participate in community service activities. We have discovered when kids get actively involved in caring about others they reap huge benefits.

In those early years we knew we wanted to teach our children about giving and to help them realize the personal benefits. As more Kids Korps volunteers went into the community to serve, wonderful things started to happen. Children, in general, became more self-assured, better able to reflect on their own and others' actions—and were more enjoyable to be around. Many became leaders in their peer groups and communities.

We learned that teaching kids to care genuinely about others seemed to inoculate them against some of the social ills we parents worry about. It made them stronger and rendered a good defense against peer pressure, lack of direction, and self-doubt, by helping them to feel valued, needed, and purposeful.

Kids' willingness and ability to understand the importance of interdependence emerged from years of observing them, their parents, and other volunteers. The children learned to bond and connect with others; to gain a broader perspective of themselves and life in general, to be grateful to life and for what they have, and to feel the power of acting on an inspired idea or moment. And then we found research—study after study—that substantiated the value of these qualities.

Caring about others—and demonstrations that show it—is a good thing for kids.

> "The values that Kids Korps instills in each of its members and participants reflect those I hope every [American] will make their own: service, respect, integrity, positive identity, and teamwork. Kids Korps volunteers are making [America] a better place for all of us to live."
>
> —Maria Shriver's Letter of Recognition to Kids Korps 2005

PART 2

Conquering the Obstacles of Healthy Development

Collecting backpacks and
school supplies for Hurricane
Katrina victims

A young volunteer shows
gratitude after a busy day.

Elementary school students
make blankets for homeless children.

An inner-city youth enjoys
a day of bowling with
Teen Korps volunteers.

3
The Five Essential Touchstones
An Overview

"One thing I know: the only ones among you who will be really happy are those who will have sought and found how to serve."

—Albert Schweitzer

I n our experience, five solid principles and related action steps have risen to the top of the list of core values that lay a firm foundation for the healthy growth of children. We call these touchstones. A touchstone, by definition, is any test of genuineness or value. As an actual stone, touchstones test the authenticity of gold or silver. Our touchstones help kids "test" themselves by giving them insight to understand their inner self more clearly, what to expect in their daily lives, and how to feel more authentically engaged and content. Twelve years of observation and plenty of research have validated using the five touchstones as a way to develop stronger and sturdier kids, by teaching your children to care. When parents incorporate these key principles, they help their children build a genuine depth of character and loving spirit. The following summarizes the touchstones:

Interdependence: the understanding that we all need one another. When families and community members reach out and pull together, they learn how to count on each other to accomplish a shared goal. Children who develop the cooperative spirit of interdependence are more likely to care about others and to have that caring returned. When they feel confident in their ability to care for and relate to others, they are more likely to stand up for what they believe in and, when needed, can take a stand against what they *don't* believe in. Working well with others aids in the development of leadership skills and social competency. This coming together and learning to depend on one another helps stave off selfishness, isolation, negative peer pressure, unhealthy self-importance, and feelings of low self-worth. When children work for the greater good, they become responsible. Their internal fortitude grows.

Connection: the ability to blend, belong, and bond. Sharing one's inner self comes more easily for some than others. When we can break down the barriers of pretense, the ability to connect with others will grow. Showing one's true self to others—and being accepted for it— enables us to form deep, rich, and rewarding relationships. Through bonding, we experience both giving and receiving with grace. Humans are hard-wired to connect, and when we do so in positive ways, we tap into our moral and spiritual selves, which develops internal sturdiness.

Children who reach out to others and build secure relationships will learn social skills, gain perspective, and develop greater empathy for others. Connection helps stave off feelings of rejection, alienation, isolation, and self-absorption. Children who connect will feel accepted, gain a sense of belonging, experience greater happiness, and have fewer behavioral problems.

Perspective: the ability to see things more clearly from different points of view. Experiencing life outside themselves makes children better able to develop understanding and compassion for others, and to have a greater tolerance for all. Perspective helps stave off insensitivity, pessimism, and feelings of entitlement and victimization. By helping children see things from other viewpoints, we help them gain tolerance and flexibility and make better decisions. They are better able to weather life's ups and downs, without magnifying them. They have a better chance for balance.

Gratitude: a deep feeling of appreciation for life's blessings. Gratitude plays a significant role in a child's sense of well-being and feeling loved. The spirit of gratitude helps children maintain a positive attitude toward themselves and others. It helps stave off misplaced priorities, hopelessness, entitlement, negativity, and jealousy. With gratitude, children feel a sense of wonder. Children with a grateful heart are more likely to experience inner joy and contentment in their lives and draw upon their soulful, spiritual nature. A child who is authentically grateful will more likely experience deep happiness and feel richly content, both of which can help them reap positive mental and physical health benefits.

Inspiration: an internal drive that ignites our desires, fires us up, and spurs us on. Inspiration helps kindle our children's curiosity and spirit of adventure, giving them a sense of excitement that may open doors to self-discovery. Inspiration staves off boredom, laziness, apathy, depression, and a false sense of self. Inspired children are spurred on by an internal passion to develop goals and create a purpose-filled, purpose-driven life.

The five touchstones increase our children's level of competence and compassion, and generate good character. We've watched youth develop a positive self-identity, a sense of purpose, and deeper connections with family and community. In our mission we set out to imbue children's hearts with the spirit of caring and giving, which—in turn—we discovered, helped them acquire terrific core values. The foundation of what we teach in Kids Korps now incorporates these values:

Service to Community

Kids quickly learn that giving to others is

- not difficult,

- a good thing to do,

- a joyous experience.

When leaving a nursing home where he and his mother had spent time helping seniors, Tommy, age ten, exclaimed, "I'm so glad we came, Mom. It makes me feel good right here." He put his hand over his heart.

He had experienced connection.

Respect for Community

Young volunteers learn

- the world does not revolve around them,

- empathy and compassion for others,

- to become more appreciative of family,

- to take responsibility for their environment.

They learn interdependence—counting on each other, giving and receiving, realizing they are a part of something bigger.

Susannah, age fifteen, expressed this well when she said, "Not only are we building a house for people in need, but we are also building friendships and strong bonds with people."

Personal Integrity

Young people who serve others become:

- honest

- courteous

- fair

- kind

- trustworthy

They have lots of courage, which comes from experiencing the inspiration to do something good.

Jarred, age fourteen, explained: "At the Special Olympics, I partnered with Tom, a twenty-four-year-old man who could not speak and had very little communication skills. To watch him get so excited to compete in the high jump or relay races and then smile out loud each time he received a ribbon was really rewarding. I think I had as much fun as he did."

Volunteers coach Special Olympics athletes and develop friendships during a track-and-field meet.

Personal Identity

Youthful volunteers discover a sense of purpose and responsibility. They gain:

- a new perspective on life

- confidence about making a difference

- increased self-esteem

- a grateful heart

Channelle, age fifteen, said, "I learned that sometimes we take for granted all the things we have every day, like food and a warm place to sleep. We should appreciate the things we have. Some people are not as fortunate. With all the troubles the world has, it's nice to know someone cares."

Leadership and Teamwork

Kids learn quickly that leadership comes from knowing how to

- connect with others,

- interact positively,

- build teams.

Young Kids Korps volunteers develop initiative and have a sense of empowerment and accomplishment. Family relationships strengthen through learning that sharing themselves and their time is an important part of giving.

After spending three days building a house for a needy family in Mexico, Ashley, age seventeen, said, "I always leave feeling completely rewarded because I know I've been an important part of a team that has provided a wonderful, deserving family with something they have been waiting for. We're giving them a place to call home."

**Teens building a
house in Mexico**

When our children are encouraged to bond with others, to work with others for common goals, to see things from others' perspective, to develop an attitude of gratitude, and to be inspired to take positive action, they become "Kids Who Care."

Raising caring kids can impact the dynamics of your family, your community, and, indeed, our world, as you will see in the many examples sprinkled throughout this book. The chapters that follow provide real-life tools for helping your children become capable and compassionate and develop good character—to become kids who care.

"It is one of the beautiful compensations of this life that no one can sincerely try to help another without helping himself."

—Charles Dudley Warner

4

The Touchstone of Interdependence

Are We Raising Kids Who
Can Depend on Each Other?

*"Each citizen should play his part
in the community according to his individual gifts."*

—Plato

Our discussion of the five touchstones begins with interdependence because we believe—and research shows—that our ability to be counted upon and to count on others builds the foundation of human health. Interdependence can extend to other individuals, communities, or even the planet.

As in most things, both positive and negative aspects prevail in interdependence. For example, street gangs and enabling relationships encourage negativity—although interdependent, they lack a positive connection. The key is knowing how to depend on one another in healthy ways for the benefit of all.

Eleven-year-old Robby had preferred not to be away from his friends for four days, especially to work in the hot sun for people he "didn't even know." He had kind of agreed to help when his mom asked, but he hadn't realized it meant giving up so many days and not being home for the Superbowl. He, his mother, and a group of other family "volunteers" had driven across the border into Mexico to help build a house for a family in need. Robby moped around the work site, dragging tools here and there, shuffling his feet in the dust and, with each hour, grew more and more preoccupied with the layers of dirt his shoes had accumulated. Even the increasing happiness of the family, as they watched their new home literally take shape, didn't change his outlook. Robby had other thoughts on his mind: Back home, his two older brothers would be getting ready for the Superbowl, a game they all looked forward to. He could already smell the popcorn and pizza. And, now he'd have to miss it.

By the second day, Robby's mood had actually worsened. "Why do we have to stay?" he pouted to his mother. "There's a whole lot of other people here to help. Why can't they finish it? We've already been here two days, and besides, you didn't make Tim and Zack come! Mom, I really want to go home. Can we, please? Pleeeease, Mom?" he pleaded. "Pleeeeease!"

Robby saw only his own difficulties—working out in the hot sun and missing the big game. He didn't truly understand the value of his time or the value of working together as a team to do something very important for a family in need.

Robby's reaction emulates that of any child faced with a task that interferes with his "due." Of course, he didn't understand the worth and potential impact of anything apart from his own circle of friends. Children tend to rebel against anything that disrupts their pleasure. How many kids actually *want* to make their bed, do their homework, or take out the garbage—much less give up an entire weekend to work for someone else's sake? They need a substantial reason to deviate from the ingrown impulse toward selfishness.

Robby's mother put him in the position of not getting his

short-term comfort needs met. He was hot, working hard, and now would have to endure the disappointment of not participating in something he looked forward to every year. Robby's mother tried to *show* her child why caring does matter, by taking him on the trip. Whether knowingly or not, she had set him up to begin to think about the needs of others.

Focusing on ourselves impedes our seeing the added dimension of the importance of depending on others, and others depending on us, or the potential joy of reaching out to others in authentic and meaningful ways. Most children understand the gratification of immediate or tangible rewards, such as money they can spend on going to the movies with their friends or buying the latest sought-after items—the hottest new CD, fad clothing, or the newest cell phone—to give them status or make them popular with their friends. But do they understand the value of giving?

By the end of that second day on the work site, as the sun was setting and the majority of the volunteers had loaded the vans and headed for dinner, Robby discovered his mother, Ellen, sweeping the cement floor of the house under construction. Tired, his mood quarrelsome, Robby absolutely did not understand why his mother lagged behind when everyone else was leaving. He watched as she swept the sawdust and particles of debris from the cement. Irritated, he asked, "Mom, why are you doing this? It'll just be a mess again tomorrow."

Patiently, his mother explained that the Rios family, with five children between the ages of one and thirteen, had been living with another family in a small and crowded place. A clean floor, tonight, would allow them to get right to work and make further progress on their new house, tomorrow.

Robby's eyes widened, and his face softened, and she could see that he better understood not only the importance of sweeping the floor, but also the urgency of completing the home for this family.

"Do you want to pick up that broom and help me sweep, so we can get to dinner, too?"

Without hesitation, Robby picked up the broom and began helping his mother.

"What room do you think you're sweeping?" his mom asked. "Do you think that will be the kitchen or a bedroom?"

Her son stopped, looked around, and replied, "I think this is a bedroom."

"Me too," she said. "There are five children, and they will have to share a bedroom."

"I'd hate to share my room with anyone!"

His mother said nothing and waited as her son again looked around the various spaces marked with two-by-fours.

Robby seemed to evaluate the small size of the bedroom. "I think the kids have to share this one." He paused, then added, "Except for maybe the baby . . ."

Ellen saw him grapple with the idea of four kids in a room. "Do you think Anthony Rios will have friends over to his new house? Do you think he watches football with his friends?" Seeing the thoughtful look in Robby's eyes, Ellen added, "If the Rios family had a television, where do you think they would put it?"

"What do you mean 'if'?" Robby asked. "How could they not have a television?"

"Some houses don't have electricity, Rob," she responded.

"Hmm . . ."

That night, in the dorm, as they got ready for bed, Robby said: "I'm glad they're getting a new house, Mom."

The next day, Robby woke early and seemed eager to get started. Quite a change from the day before. And, through the day he did a lot of talking with Anthony.

For the next two days, Robby worked harder than his mom had ever seen. Along with the other volunteers, he cheerfully carried windows and drywall and, later, on his knees, he nailed floorboards in what would be the kitchen.

In the car on the way home Robby relayed some of his conversations with Anthony. "He doesn't go to school all the time. He wants to, but sometimes he has to watch his brother and sisters because he's the oldest and both of his parents work."

"It's good that we helped the Rios family build their house," Ellen said without really expecting a response.

Robby had one anyway. "I think it's awesome we helped them, Mom. Do you think Anthony can go to school more now?"

"I hope so, Rob. I think it would mean a lot to him. I learned something else this weekend. Now that Anthony's family has a cement floor instead of the dirt one they had, illness can be cut down by as much as 50 percent. If the kids don't get sick, Anthony won't have to watch them as much."

"Wow . . ." Robby thought for a moment, then blurted out: "Can we buy Anthony a computer? He doesn't have one."

"I'm sure there are lots of kids like Anthony who don't have the great things you have, like a computer or a TV. And, do you know that kids like Anthony live right in our own town?"

Robby's eyes got big. "There is a kid at school who sometimes doesn't have lunch money and so doesn't eat lunch. And . . ."

That first night back home, Robby obviously felt good about himself, as he excitedly shared his stories with his brothers. His mom smiled at her middle son's reaction. The sometimes-sulky fourteen-year-old had put up such a skirmish about going, his mother had decided against taking him. But now, he said, "I want to go the next time you build a house for someone . . ."

The Touchstone of Interdependence

Embodied in the skill of interdependence is the willingness of a child to work with others to accomplish a shared goal, and the ability to work harmoniously in a group to that end. But willingness and ability don't always go hand in hand. Most children are *able* to set the table or clean their rooms, but are they *willing?* Parents must encourage willingness while building competency in their children. Just like Robby's mother, we need to provide our children with safe but challenging opportunities through which they can develop the skills we're trying to teach and the *willingness* to use those skills for the good of others.

When our children value working with and for others, it can help resolve some of the concerns that parents and society have about, and for, today's youth.

Renowned psychologist Lawrence Kohlberg studied how people develop a sense of right, wrong, justice, and regard for human welfare as they mature. Through observation and testing, he developed an influential theory suggesting that children go through sequential stages of reasoning as they develop ethically and morally. Kohlberg believed that moral education requires individual reflection and experience. With this, adults and children can become moral agents in their communities. Helping kids learn to cooperate and to understand their interdependence with others sets them up to think about how their decisions can make a difference and to know they are not acting in isolation—a sign, according to Kohlberg, of moral maturity.

Kohlberg's Stages of Moral Development

Through the following stages, moral decisions are driven by maturational ability. According to Kohlberg, the stages occur sequentially. The first stage applies to children up until about age ten. The remaining stages are arrived at after age ten through adulthood.[1]

1. Premoral or Preconventional Morality

   Stage 1—Punishment and obedience: doing what you're told under threat of punishment or anticipation of pleasure.

   Stage 2—Individualism and exchange: "You scratch my back; I'll scratch yours." Decisions are based on individual interests.

2. Conventional Morality

   Stage 3—Interpersonal conformity: doing right according to the expectations of one's social group, to gain approval from others. Also, developing one's own ideas of a good person, based on opinions that are important to one.

   Stage 4—Law and social order: driven by respect for rules and laws according to a constituted authority.

3. Postconventional or Principled Morality

Stage 5—Prior rights and social contract: ethical decisions made based on the rights and welfare of the individual needing protection from society. Logic, as opposed to a checklist of rules, governs decisions.

Stage 6—Universal ethical principles: ethical decisions made based on the equality and worth of all human beings.

What motivates your child in making decisions and solving problems about right and wrong? According to Kohlberg, children arrive at stages of moral decision-making in a developmental fashion. Your expectations of a ten-year-old's capabilities differ from what you anticipate from a five-year-old. For example, the younger child will most likely make a decision based on avoiding pain and gaining something pleasurable for himself. "I'll be good if you give me a cookie" may be a familiar sentiment delivered, with or without words, by your little one. Your ten-year-old will more likely base his moral decisions on what his friends are doing—and what they are getting away with—because he wants to fit in.

Based on Kohlberg's work, many adults never make it to the highest level of moral decision-making, where people internalize their standards and reasoning about right and wrong through abstract thinking and grounded ethical principles. What parent doesn't want her child to develop the skills to make good moral and ethical decisions? We believe, through the five touchstones in this book—starting with interdependence—we can raise kids destined to understand and embrace higher-order ethics. Climbing the ladder of moral development takes experience and maturity, but the more "good" we can put into our children, the more steadily they will climb.

Why Interdependence Is a Good Thing for Your Child: Six Key Benefits

When we help our children develop a healthy sense of interdependence, it not only benefits them but society, as well. Kids who possess an interdependent spirit tend to care about others and to be cared about by them. Working well with others contributes to increased feelings of social mastery, which aids in honing leadership skills and results in seeing oneself as responsible. In short, internal fortitude grows, and children become what therapists call "psychologically hardy."

Through our experience with Kids Korps, we've learned how cooperating with others helps children problem solve and, thus, promotes teamwork. In so doing they will gain six benefits:

1. A belief in their own abilities. Children who see themselves as helpful will more likely gain a solid sense of mastery. They know they have the capacity to *do*, and to *succeed*. Those who feel worthy and capable in their ability to develop positive relationships undoubtedly stand up for what they believe in—and stand against what they *don't* believe in. Even in childhood, people need to stand their ground—sometimes difficult when they may be a lone voice or have an unpopular stance. Internal strength is a vital ingredient in resisting or succumbing to negative peer pressure and enables children to act on a better or more positive alternative.

2. Higher self-esteem. Children who feel useful and needed also gain confidence in meeting others' needs. Seeing themselves as "good"—and knowing how much the good they do matters—naturally makes kids feel better about themselves and their lives in general. Learning how to function as an integral part of a team brings internal satisfaction and reduces self-destructive behaviors. When children see themselves as willing and able participants in something that benefits the greater good, the reflection in the mirror is a "good" one, and thus makes a child better able to like the face he or she sees in the mirror. Being on friendly terms with the face in the mirror not only greatly reduces self-destructive behaviors, but also increases a child's desire to feel again the positive reinforcement that comes with caring about and doing for others.

3. A greater willingness to accept responsibility. Knowing others depend on them helps children "show up" to a situation or relationship. It helps them set an internal compass to value being there for others—to help, support, and assist when it's needed. They can then take personal responsibility for positive outcomes.

4. A willingness to lead. Interdependence aids in the development of social skills and creates a sense of responsibility for others that can result in a willingness to lead. Children gain an understanding of how to enlist others to accomplish a task and, through this, become comfortable in taking a lead role in decision-making. They will develop into the kind of leaders who, when called upon, act fairly and confidently.

5. A strong support system. Depression in children greatly concerns parents these days. Isolation is a key indicator for depression. When children discover the satisfaction—even joy—of working with others, they feel less lonely and less alone. No longer isolated from the goodwill and support they can both give and receive, they realize when times get rough, they are not alone in the world. In turn, they will reach out to others, in support, when needed.

6. A greater sense of purpose. When children can balance their needs with the needs of others, they feel more confident about their purpose in the world. They know and understand the value of their efforts.

Of course, we should let our kids know that putting their own needs first and having a single-minded focus is at times appropriate. But they must also know when to step outside themselves and look out for others—one of the most important skills we can encourage them to develop.

My college-age daughter has such a lovely sense of caring and compassion for others. And from watching and listening, I can see that this quality draws others to her. I'm always amazed to see how much others simply like and want to be around her. And they are quick to place her in leadership roles—and readily follow her lead. If she feels something is important and worth doing, others will get on board. It's amazing to me to see how others just trust her. I think they feel that if she looks out for the good of others, then they will receive the same treatment. And who doesn't want to be around someone with this mindset? I'm proud that she values people in the way that she does. By bringing out the best in others, by wanting the best for them, it is as though she has ensured her own sense of community, which will look out for her in return.

—Mary Louise, parent

Helping Children "Get" the Lesson: The "Aha Shift"

Children like feeling needed. It enhances their self worth, and their spirits grow when they know others can depend on them.

Sometimes, a light bulb switches on and tells them they're appreciated. Other times kids need a little nudging to "get" the lesson.

Certainly, we want all six benefits of a spirit of interdependence for our children. So how can we help them develop that spirit? We must put into place parenting actions that produce solid results. As we've learned in our work over the years, children best learn interdependence from firsthand experience. Parents should create opportunities for building or enhancing in their children a genuine and authentic sense of caring for others.

Four Ways to Instill a Spirit of Interdependence in Your Child

1. **Model the behavior you want your child to emulate.** Whenever you can, teach by example. Children learn by watching others, especially their parents. Modeling interdependence and caring for others teaches your children to include working together with others in their journey through life. They learn how their family assists, supports, and cares about other people. Parents teach this by showing children the importance of listening carefully and thoughtfully, and responding to needs by helping others. When you do something for a neighbor, friend, or community member, let your children see you do it. When appropriate, have them share in the experience with you.

2. **Talk about the importance of cooperating with and caring about others.** This can call attention to the various ways we depend on one another. Ask your children questions such as, *Why is it important for our family to work together to keep our home neat and clean? Why is it important to care about and look out for a sibling? Why is it important to ask others about themselves, or extend a smile or a kind word when someone else seems down, even if that person isn't a close friend? Why is it important to help someone at school, such as a new student who needs to feel welcome? Why is it important to help the elderly?*

Help your children to reflect on how they reach out. Catch your children helping and let them know you value these actions. (See

"Conversation Starters" at the end of this chapter for more questions to discuss with your children.)

3. Provide your child with opportunities to interact with others in helping-out settings. Kids need to know they have the ability to step outside themselves. Show them how to assist at home, school, and in their communities. Clean up the grounds of a park where you picnic or take them on a community work project, such as planting a community tree. Strive to involve them in team-building experiences. Being on a sports team or participating in extracurricular activities can help build a mindset of working together and looking out for others, too. Provide opportunities for your children to emerge from isolating activities and engage in activities with others.

Even a young child can enjoy planting a tree to help beautify a neighborhood.

4. Help your child "think globally but act locally." Teach your children how to take what they learn from these outreach experiences and apply those techniques to other situations. Brainstorm with them on ways they can help others at their school, at home, or in the community. For example, when Robby returned from his experience of building a house for a family in Mexico, how might he have taken that experience and applied it to helping others in his home, at school, or in his community? The benefits of good works are transferable, so teach children to see the big picture.

"It's not enough to have lived. We should be determined to live for something. May I suggest that it be creating joy for others, sharing what we have for the betterment of personkind, bringing hope to the lost and love to the lonely."

—Leo Buscaglia

How Robby's Mother Made a Difference

Robby's story is similar to others we hear about time and time again in our work with Kids Korps, as we help kids fully engage in learning about interdependence. For some families, helping, supporting, assisting, and looking out for others comes as second nature. For others, it requires a conscious effort. Of course, it's both absolutely essential and enjoyable to spend time doing things together as a family; but also important is teaching your kids to learn the value in caring for and about others, and instilling the willingness and ability to do so.

Robby's mother did five key things to lead Robby to internalize the importance of being part of a team that helps others and to understand the value of participation. She

1. made the experience happen;

2. insisted on his participation and showed him, through her example, the importance of helping;

3. talked to him about what they hoped to accomplish, and why;

4. encouraged him to evaluate his situation;

5. talked about the experience after they left and, literally, brought the lessons home.

By exposing him to a situation where he had an opportunity to help others, she encouraged her son to expand his awareness of the human need to depend on one another. Through this interaction, Robby gained a greater belief in his own abilities, increased his self-esteem, developed a greater willingness to accept responsibility, and began to grow a willingness to lead others. And as he developed his own resolve, his short-term desires took a backseat. But something more happened for Robby in the alchemy of giving: The experience reached his heart. Subsequently, Robby will most likely reach out again and, probably, get others to join him.

How Interdependent Is Your Child?

1) How often do you talk with your kids about the importance of working with others?
   a. frequently
   b. occasionally
   c. never

2) Do people ever comment on your child's giving nature?
   a. frequently
   b. occasionally
   c. never

3) How often do you volunteer or extend yourself to others?
   a. frequently
   b. occasionally
   c. never

4) When you do reach out to others, do you talk about it with your kids?
   a. on a regular basis
   b. when I have the time
   c. never

5) When was the last time you and your child became involved in a community project or did something nice for a friend or neighbor in need?

    a. in the past few months

    b. a few years ago

    c. never

Making Interdependent Caring a Part of Everyday Life

You can raise the level of cooperation and interdependence in your kids. We encourage you to involve your children in doing something big for others in a positive way. But don't wait; start now. Caring for others can become a way of life for those *you* care about.

To aid in developing your children's willingness to care about and to look out for others, consider trying some of the following.

If you have 3 minutes . . . Tell—and show—your child the importance of . . .

- offering a smile and making eye contact, when saying thank you;

- holding open the door for someone else;

- giving the right of way to others in line or when appropriate;

- offering a pregnant woman or senior your seat, when need be.

If you have 30 minutes . . . Assist your child in . . .

- bringing flowers or other gifts to someone in need of cheering up;

- creating and mailing a letter to a shut-in;

- doing little household chores, such as setting the table and cleaning up together as a family;

- establishing "table talk" whereby everyone at the table gets to share something about his or her day;

- talking about people in your community on whom you depend, such as nurses, doctors, police officers, and teachers.

If you have 3 hours . . . As a family . . .

- deliver meals to homebound individuals;

- clean up the beach or park with your kids and plan a cookout afterward;

- decorate goodie bags filled with doggie and kitty treats, and take them to your neighborhood animal shelter;

- visit a local nursing home to interact with the seniors (play games, read books, etc.);

- bake cookies or bring donuts to firefighters or police officers;

- make a list and take turns doing the more time-consuming chores around the house;

- walk dogs for neighbors.

If you have 3 days . . . As a family . . .

- work with local charities building homes, or other community services;

- take a weekend trip and plan service opportunities along the way: clean beaches and parks, visit animal shelters or nursing homes;

- become a "buddy" family for a child with special needs;

- plan a bake sale or car wash with your neighborhood and use the proceeds to buy things for kids in need;

- organize a neighborhood garage sale, then use the funds raised to beautify your neighborhood; for example, enlist the neighbors to help plant trees or start a community garden for all families to enjoy.

Developing compassion for neglected animals at a local shelter

Young volunteers team up to remove invasive plants from a preserve.

Conversation Starters for Parents and Children

Talk to your children, on a regular basis, about working with others and cooperating. Some questions to help you get the ball rolling in starting a dialogue with your child about learning interdependence:

- What do you like most about sharing? What makes it hard for you to share?

- How did you go out of your way to help someone today? Why did you help?

- What are some ways you depend on other people for your own well-being? What ways do people depend on you?

- What are some reasons you might not cooperate? Are there times when it's a good thing *not* to join in?

- Are there some areas of your life where you can do a better job of working with others—helping them and letting them help you?

- What activity can we plan as a family that will help us to better share with others?

- Whom do you admire because he or she often does something for others?

"The volunteer has become a major force in our lives because it is not possible for a man to live separated from others. We are involved in each other's lives not by choice but by necessity."

—Nils Schweizer

5

The Touchstone of Connection

The Importance of Blending, Bonding, and Belonging

"A candle loses nothing of its light when lighting another."

—Kahlil Gibran

Miles had a good relationship with his family at home, but he didn't have many friends at school. He didn't wear the latest sneakers or have the "hot" brand of backpack. He had no cell phone or MP3 player. And, to make matters worse, he stuttered. This condition caused him to shy away from conversation, which resulted in many of his classmates avoiding him.

Carlton, on the other hand, had a tumultuous relationship with his family. With an older brother and two younger, he found he could get more attention and keep his brothers "in line"—even the oldest—by making them fear him.

Carlton belittled Miles every chance he got: by jeering, smirking, or name-calling. Whatever the shortcoming of the moment—Miles's stuttering, clothes, or merely his presence—Carlton found every opportunity to keep Miles at the center of his putdowns and the butt of his jokes. For example, if the bus were overcrowded, with the only open seat next to Miles, Carlton would laugh and taunt the kid who had to sit there. Of course, this ridicule then made it difficult for Miles's seatmate to fit in with others.

Because of Miles's general shyness, the kids viewed him as passive—a kid who wouldn't fight back or even stand up for himself—until one pivotal day.

One afternoon, Carlton was standing at his locker with a group of friends when Miles came walking down the hall. Seizing the opportunity at the sight of Miles, Carlton said loudly, "Has a-a-a-a-an-n-n-n-n-y-one seee-ee-eeen-nnn Mi-i-i-i-iles today?" Then laughing loudly and looking in the direction of Miles, he said, "Oh, there he is!"

Instead of letting Carlton's comments pass, as he had so many times before, Miles dropped his books and charged at Carlton, knocking him down. Carlton, wide-eyed, stood and pushed Miles, who then pushed in return. A teacher stopped the interchange and both boys landed in the principal's office and received reprimands. When they left his office, the boys scowled at each other.

A few weeks later, the school scheduled a class trip to a shelter for abandoned children. Miles complained to his mother, "I don't want to go."

He hadn't told her he feared Carlton, but she knew about the bullying from having interacted with his teachers. She responded by telling him to concentrate on giving his best to the kids at the shelter. "Think about what you can give them," she urged. "Those kids need you. Let them see what a nice person you are. You'll have fun."

The school had called Carlton's house enough times to worry his dad. "Think about how you'd feel if kids were teasing you," he said.

"Yeah, right, Dad," Carlton retorted. "They wouldn't dare!" He hesitated. "One kid, Miles, did push me a while back. But, he's really a stuttering jerk."

"Do you ever think about how Miles feels when you make fun of him?" Carlton's dad asked.

"He's used to it, Dad. It's not like I'm the only one who teases him. We all do it." He shrugged and rolled his eyes. "He is not cool."

"Did you know, someone interviewed that football player you admire, and he said he was an outsider in high school? Would you say he isn't cool, Carlton?"

"Of course not, Dad. But I just can't imagine Miles becoming like him!"

This first scenario often gets played out between kids—some excluded, others, like Miles, targeted—merely because they are "different" or don't easily blend into a group. And we pray it doesn't happen to our kids.

But, the Carltons of the world have their own set of problems. Kids like Carlton crave being the center of attention and often try to achieve it at someone else's expense. They lack empathy for others' feelings, and their own level of connection with their groups has little depth, because it's a false connection, largely based on their ability to amuse their peers. If this type of situation goes unchecked, it can breed dangerously high levels of negative emotion, such as the case with Miles.

On the day of the class trip, when the bus drove into the gated yard of the shelter, the homeless children stood eagerly waiting for the "big kids."

As soon as Miles and the others got out of the bus, all the little kids came running up, trying to get picked up for piggyback rides.

Miles noticed one little kid in particular because he stood off to the side and just stared. He looked like he didn't trust any of the older school kids. Miles liked him right away because he could totally understand his attitude.

They got a tour of the shelter, and the kids showed them their rooms, all with bunk beds. Miles kept watching the shy kid, who stayed in the back of the group throughout the tour. At one point, Miles went over to him and said, "Hello" and learned his name . . . Charlie. The boy looked past Miles, to his watch. When Miles smiled, Charlie quickly looked away. But, every now and then he'd again glance over at the watch. So, the next time Charlie looked his way, Miles let him try it on. Charlie gave him a huge smile. Miles decided to let him wear it for a while.

After lunch they started a singalong. Charlie and Miles sat in the back, sort of watching things. Then one of the counselors asked if anyone wanted to join in. Some of the guys from school had brought instruments and Miles had his guitar with him. So he grabbed his guitar case and took Charlie up to the front where they started playing and singing. Everybody was totally into it, and Miles realized that even Carlton had joined in!

The day went fast for Miles. Then, as he put his guitar away, he noticed that all of the little boys had circled around Charlie.

Pointing in Miles's direction, Charlie said to the other boys, "He gave it to me!"

All heads turned to look at Miles and then back at the watch Charlie wore. Of course Miles hadn't planned to give it to him, but seeing how happy he was, he heard himself saying, "It's for you, Charlie." He laughed. "It's YOUR watch now."

Charlie smiled, and tears welled up in his eyes. "It's mine," he said. "It's all mine."

Carlton was in the group of kids watching Charlie and Miles. And then, when they were getting on the bus, Carlton came up to Miles and said, "Hey, dude, I didn't know you could sing! And where'd you learn to play like that?" Then he added, "I saw what you did for that kid."

"Yeah, I guess he got attached to my watch," Miles said.

"No, I mean what you did made him feel good. Why did you do it?"

Miles was really surprised, because Carlton actually sounded kind of nice. He responded, "I thought Charlie was a scared little kid who didn't expect to be treated well." Miles smiled broadly.

Carlton said nothing on the drive back, but when he walked down the aisle to get off the bus, he leaned over and spoke to Miles. Instead of spouting his usual negative comments, he asked Miles if he wanted to play ball the next week.

Before Miles could do more than nod, the guy behind him said to get a move on, so they shuffled out the door.

Later, Miles told his mom, "I can't believe I didn't want to go on that trip. It was such a great day. I have a feeling, Mom, that Carlton won't be making fun of me anymore."

Miles and Carlton resolved their differences and "connected." But of course, the more desirable thing is for the problem not to have initiated in the first place. So how do we help our children to learn empathy while acquiring the skills to blend in, to belong, and to bond—in healthy and appropriate ways? How can we prevent our children from becoming outcasts like Miles—or bullies like

Carlton? How can we protect them from the anger, anxiety, and depression that often result in exclusion from "the group?"

The Touchstone of Connection

Generation after generation, kids work hard to blend in with their peers. Most children—from their first day of kindergarten on through high-school graduation—don't want to feel left out. They will go overboard to fit in with their peer group. No kid wants to be the last one chosen for a schoolyard game, sit at home instead of going to the prom, or be left out of any group gathering. To belong, though, children need to see themselves as capable of—and worthy of—friendships. And gaining the confidence to reach out to others begins in the inner circle of family. As parents, we must teach them to have empathy and to act and react kindly.

As children grow and mature, they become more susceptible to the influence of others, both positive and negative, in an effort to define themselves. One of our jobs as parents includes helping children develop a healthy and positive ability to connect to others, teaching them how to build trustworthy relationships—and how to return that trust. This learned behavior molds healthy lives.

As children learn what it means to belong, they more aptly develop healthy bonds. The bonding we hope for our children grows from their ability to establish deep, rich, and rewarding relationships—by showing their true selves to others and gaining acceptance. Children who befriend others have stronger feelings of belonging, experience a sense of appreciation for one another, and grow in their ability to empathize. Strong social connections will help them throughout life—in friendships, school, work, and love.

True bonding with others goes a step beyond merely sharing experiences. Bonding happens when people feel empathy and compassion for one another. Have you noticed how people who manage to have positive social connections understand how to blend and how to belong? They have developed the necessary empathy and understanding to really care for and stand by others, to embrace friends, siblings, and parents unconditionally—warts and all. Bonding comes through developing and *nurturing* relationships.

One night, instead of eating out, our family went downtown together to serve meals to the homeless. My kids didn't realize how grateful and kind the people they served food to would be. And me? I was almost in tears watching my children be so attentive and giving to others. All of us were touched by our experience. I don't remember every evening we have gone out to dinner, but that one night sure stayed with me. We helped create a new language of caring in our family. That night we all felt good about ourselves, and three years later…we still use that experience to talk about the gifts of giving.

—Cheri, parent

Children who can genuinely connect with others will more likely come to "know" people. Seeing people for who they really are—not as society paints them—makes developing true personal connections much easier. That ability to relate to people on a more realistic level allows children to see themselves more realistically, as well. In stereotyping or judging others less, they judge themselves less.

Are Today's Kids on a Shorter Fuse?

Kids establish their own social pecking order. This is nothing new. Through the years, parents and teachers have attempted to guide the power plays and social struggles of youth by modeling community involvement, molding character, and teaching ethics. Of course, we've always had to deal with bullies like Carlton, but the number of bullies—and victims—who become volatile has grown dramatically in recent times. Doesn't it seem that many of today's children have a short fuse? Certainly, the increase in violent video games and kids' access to every conceivable thing on the Internet promote aggressive behavior. Many children today have misplaced values. They see violent actions as commonplace, even natural.

It doesn't help that 4 to 20 percent of kids between ages nine and fourteen are latchkey kids—home alone to fend for themselves—unmonitored, with few rules. This can result in isolated play. Exposure to violence through the media, video games, entertainment industry, etc., plays an increasing part in molding their lives. Kids have always tried to copy those they regard as role models, whether peers, parents, other adults, celebrities, sports stars, or music groups. What models do we give our kids today? Children need to experience relationships with others in order to develop empathy, compassion, and consideration—and to get back the same. The mixed messages children receive these days make it harder and harder to instill those values.

Why are kids so vulnerable to dangerous influences? For one reason, they feel a need to belong; in fact, according to some experts, we are hard-wired to connect. This is the key: When children—even in the wake of difficult experiences—feel connected, rather than alienated from others, they tend not to lash out in aggressive ways. But feeling alone, alienated, or rejected lights a short fuse—sometimes with devastating consequences. Consider the April 20, 1999, Columbine High School shooting. Dylan Klebold and Eric Harris opened fire in their school cafeteria in Littleton, Colorado. After yelling out, "All jocks stand up!" they proceeded to kill twelve classmates and one teacher, wound twenty-one, and then take their own lives. Based on their journals and the accounts of those who knew them, they were outcasts. Although Dylan and Eric appeared to be friends, the increasing anger toward their classmates—and not any sort of positive bond—forged the connection.

It's difficult to fathom the violence Dylan Klebold and Eric Harris perpetrated that day. They had grown up in middle-class families and, on the surface, seemed like average kids. Especially frightening: The boys actually planned their killing spree and justified it as a "get-back" for being made to feel like they didn't belong.

We can't just dismiss Dylan and Eric as terribly angry teenagers. We must hope that kids who meet with rejection by their peers will not boil over to the point of harming others. But, according to news reports, kids step over that line more often these days. Subsequently, parents and teachers now pay closer attention to the behavior of bullies.

At what point do feelings of not belonging plant the seeds that grow into anger, and at what point does this internal rage overwhelm children, putting them over the edge? *"If I can't belong, you don't get to either."*

One of the most important things we can do to help children is to weave a web of connection that supports them. When they do feel like outcasts—depressed, angry, lonely, or confused—established bonds can help them to reach out and get the support they need.

Outcasts and popular kids are separate entities—but not opposites. According to a 1998 study of 727 seventh and eighth graders, popular kids most often acted dominant, aggressive, stuck-up and—were not necessarily liked.[1] From the study's perspective, the popular jocks who taunted Klebold and Harris could hardly be called well-adjusted children. Based on this, ensuring that our children feel connected to others and possess the interior skills of empathy and genuine kindness has nothing to do with their gaining popularity. The study found that "popular" kids, with the trendy clothing and latest tech gadgets, often displayed negative risk-taking behavior, whereas kids described by their peers as "well-liked" had positive traits and were considered "kind and trustworthy"—but not necessarily popular.

So why are kids less likely to bond and connect today? According to the Commission of Children at Risk, unacceptably high rates of mental and behavioral problems plague our children. (Twenty-one percent of kids between age nine and seventeen have diagnosable disorders.) The commission reports: In the midst of unprecedented material affluence, kids fail to flourish. In large measure, a lack of connecting has caused this crisis of American childhood. The two kinds of connectedness, 1) getting close to other people and 2) grounding into a deep moral and spiritual meaning,[2] both play a huge part in healthy development.

Sociologist Robert Putnam, in his book *Bowling Alone,* discusses the sharp decline in the social infrastructure of American communities since the 1960s. New research shows the continuing trend: The number of people with whom the average American can discuss "important matters" has dropped by one-third, in just the last two decades. In an article in *Time* (June 2006), Putnam stated, "The big problem is social isolation, which has many well-documented side effects. Kids fail to thrive. Crime rises. Politics coarsens. Generosity shrivels. Death comes sooner. (Social isolation is as big a risk for premature death as smoking.) Well-connected people live longer, happier lives, even if they have to forgo a new Lexus to spend time with friends."[3]

It's surprising to learn that both feelings of social isolation and physical pain stimulate some of the same areas of the brain.

A UCLA study looked at the brain's reactions to social rejection and came up with interesting results. Subjects played a computer ball-tossing game, designed by researchers to exclude them from interaction. The subjects—university students—were led to believe their opponents were other students; but, actually, a computer-generated game randomly played with, and then excluded, the human subjects. Technicians took brain scans while the students played. After getting snubbed by the computerized game, the scan showed increased activity in the area of the brain (the anterior cingulated cortex) linked to physical pain.[4] Humans' powerful instincts lead them to avoid social exclusion. This makes sense as a survival value because connection helps families and societies thrive.

"The greatest of all sorrows is to feel alone, to feel unwanted, deprived of all affection."

—Mother Teresa

So what can we do to ensure that our own children do not feel alone or isolated? How can we inoculate our children against becoming overly aggressive toward others when they feel they haven't received their fair share of friendship and attention? When we look deeply into our crystal balls, what signs tell us our children are happy and connected to their peer groups in positive and healthy ways? How does feeling like an outcast—alone, and alienated from activities—affect a young person's willingness and ability to care about others? At what point do isolation and bully tactics lead youths to harm themselves and others? Why does feeling connected to others lead to positive feelings in our children?

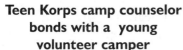

Teen Korps camp counselor bonds with a young volunteer camper

Young kids have fun packing food for low-income seniors.

Building Strong Connections: Five Key Benefits

Teaching our children how to bond with others will develop their connection skills, allowing them to form healthy attachments to others and granting them a much longed-for sense of belonging. The ability to bond in positive ways aids children in developing "relationship confidence." They know that others matter to them, and they matter to others.

1. A deeper sense of happiness. Children who have an ample supply of positive social relationships will more likely find contentment. They are much happier and feel more cared for than those who have no network of family and friends in their camp. Feeling happy and cared for promotes caring and support to others in return.

2. Healthy relationships. When our kids learn how to interact harmoniously, they are investing in healthy relationships and goodwill. Healthy relationships are based on trust, consideration, and kindness. By helping our children take steps toward making positive connections, our children will better understand how to bond and make friends.

3. Social intelligence. When children learn how to reach out and connect, they develop the ability to relate well to others. In his book *Emotional Intelligence,* Daniel Goleman writes of the value of understanding people and knowing how to relate to the social situation at hand. Social intelligence is not about our children's physical or academic abilities, but rather their ability to relate to other people.

4. Deeper friendships. Childhood can be a challenging time for establishing friendships with depth—relationships where children share confidences and ideas, as well as fears and insecurities with someone they can trust. As children learn the steps that move them toward more wholesome connections, they learn how to establish relationships where they can count on others and be counted on—a two-way street that meets both parties' needs. They are happy when their friends are happy, and vice versa. Over time, through good and bad, children who learn the value of deeper friendships are more likely to help each other *unconditionally*.

5. A sense of safety. Children who feel connected to others will more likely feel safe, knowing they have someone to turn to when they feel emotionally insecure or physically afraid. A true friend will stand by to protect you at night, in a park, or in crowds. "I've got your back" is not just a phrase; it is a declaration of mental and physical protection. Safety means shared secrets and depending on someone to be there for you, "no matter what."

Helping Children "Get" the Lesson: The "Aha Shift"

The story about Miles and Carlton (at the beginning of this chapter) clearly showed a lack of empathy and concern for others on Carlton's part—as well as a lack of courage in the other kids who apathetically watched Carlton prey on Miles. Certainly, we can't (and shouldn't) fight all our children's battles for them. But we can teach our children how to *react* in such situations.

Some kids seem to be born with an extroverted personality that helps them to develop social ties but, for the most part, children need guidance in learning how to connect with others in healthy ways. Through example, parents can teach their children the skills they need to build social connections and a sense of belonging.

Five Ways to Teach Children How to Connect and Bond with Others

1. Teach and model humanitarianism. We want our children to develop empathy toward others and for themselves . . . the best way for them to enjoy true connection. So how do we teach our children to empathize? Through humanitarianism. Concern for human welfare is the crux of humanitarianism, which is the giving side of connection. In other words, humanitarianism connects people through acts of kindness. Let your children see you taking dinner to the neighbor who just had a baby, or ask them to help you shovel the driveway for an elderly friend. Talk with them about how these actions make others feel cared for. The goal is to *show* our children the importance of valuing and treating others in caring ways. We want them to see that our actions are focused and intentional—and catch us in the act of caring. As families, we can be active in the community. Whether we work with our children to rake a neighbor's yard, organize a group to whitewash sidewalks and walls, or read stories to young children at Sunday school, the goal is to teach our children to reach out and connect with others. The bonus is how close we will grow to one another.

2. Discuss the joy in empathetic relationships. Deep connections and bonding happen when children develop the awareness, ability, and willingness to understand and respond to what others might feel, as well as to recognize and accept what their friends give them. We can talk with our children about our friendships and how much they mean to us. Tell them stories about what you do with your friends: travel, play sports, laugh together. Don't assume they understand what friendship is. Talk to them about it. Share your appreciation of others with them. You can increase your children's awareness through questions about what makes a friend a friend. Are their friends nice, honest, and trustworthy? Can they count on their friends? Do they like to give and receive? Do they bring out the best in people? Do they enjoy being with people?

3. Teach your children to find their own identity and strengths. Because children want to blend and belong, it can sometimes be difficult for them to develop relationships based on who they are. We can ask our children questions about how they view their talents and personality strengths, and we can point out the special things that we and their friends see in them. Praise them for all positive reactions. Children need to be encouraged to develop their sense of identity, and to understand their unique skills and talents, and not to adopt a false persona they feel will help them fit in. When they know their strengths, they bring something special to their relationships.

4. Help children uncover the reasons for inappropriate social behavior. When you see or hear about a child being teased, ask, "What could you do to make her feel better?" and "If you were being teased, what would you want someone to say to you or do for you?" We can help our children understand underlying motives for behavior. On the surface, a bully may appear just to be a nasty kid, but perhaps he's really expressing his loneliness in an inappropriate way. Encourage kids to look beneath the surface to understand others.

5. Strengthen family connections. A child's natural curiosity about how relationships work—why some kids are kind and some are not—can help parents guide children to become empathetic. Make them feel comfortable around us, knowing they can ask for advice and answers about relationships. "Families that play together stay together." Make traditions part of your family life. They help build a strong family bond. How do we learn to *enjoy* each other? Make time for bonding opportunities such as sharing meals, playing games, and family outings, where togetherness is the main goal. Have group discussions and family meetings to talk about common goals. Also, address issues in the spirit of goodwill and, when possible, resolve them for the good of all.

Personality Traits Can Influence How Children Interact with Others

Introvert vs. Extrovert: Is your child by nature an introvert or an extrovert? Don't use his social patterns to answer this question. Instead, watch how your child *rebuilds* his energy—with a good book or at a party? A natural introvert may act social, but when it's time to recharge, he heads for a quiet space. An extroverted counterpart may enjoy the solitude of a good book, but he gathers energy when he's with a social group. Your introverted child may connect with others by establishing only a few close friends . . . and feel bad that she doesn't "know" everyone like her extroverted counterpart. Or your extrovert may secretly feel, while she knows everyone, she is close to no one. Learning about who your child is, and helping her understand herself on this continuum, will help her establish meaningful connections. For example, a child who is introverted by nature will probably have few friends he can depend on if he is being true to himself, while an extro-verted kid will have many more extended relationships. Both are okay. As a parent, don't judge—our kids do enough judging on their own. One person is not better than another. It is a matter of how your child best connects with others. Helping your child understand his style of connecting gives him the opportunity to make his own decisions about his choices in life.

Leader vs. Follower: In general, does your child like to take charge of or follow the group? Some children are natural leaders, and some are natural followers. This is not a hard and fast claim, but rather an oppor-tunity to explore where their general comfort level lies. Thinking about both is a way for parents to explore their child's nature. Children who support others' leadership generally have come to understand them-selves and can be very good friends. Children who tend to lead seem to easily share ideas with others and can also be very good friends. It is important to guide your child in establishing confidence in either role. This confidence in "who they are" helps them to connect with others.

Optimist vs. Pessimist: Do your children see their glass as half full or half empty? Certain kids are more optimistic and others more pes-simistic, by nature. Some kids approach a task with confidence, while others shy away, get anxious, or just feel sure they can't do it.

An optimistic child tends to have regard for the positive qualities they see in themselves and others. For some children, a generally positive attitude is inherent. Parents can praise the ways their children think when they act optimistically and also model by finding the best in their own life situations. And, we can help guide children who seem inclined toward pessimism without criticizing their nature.

Parents can share stories of optimism with their kids, from preschool's *Little Engine That Could* ("I think I can" turns into "I know I can") to grammar school's *Pollyanna* (a young girl with infectious optimism), to high school's *The Miracle Worker* (Helen Keller's transition).

We can teach optimism by setting an example. If we can see the best in situations, kids will be inclined to follow suit. Children who are, or who learn to be, optimistic will probably share satisfying connections with others. And, as a bonus, in most cases, others are drawn to a pos-itive attitude.

How Miles's and Carlton's Parents Made a Difference

Both Miles's and Carlton's parents talked to their children about how to treat others. Carlton's dad planted a seed in Carlton's mind that perhaps Miles wasn't so different from other kids. Although Carlton seemed to resist his father's perspective at first, when Carlton saw Miles connecting with the little boy, playing guitar, and singing with the group, he changed his attitude. Miles's mother also did the right thing by encouraging her son to react to Carlton's taunts in a new way and not avoid his company.

When children feel conflicted, parents instinctively want to jump in and "fix" the situation. Instead, Carlton's and Miles's parents knew that encouragement would better serve their children and influence them in resolving the conflict themselves. While parenting, they needed only to keep a watchful eye.

How Socially Adjusted Is Your Child?

Ask yourself the following questions about your child:

1. Does your child seem to have an excessive desire to be popular? Get him to talk about what popularity means to him. Explain that popularity doesn't usually come from deep, meaningful friendships, but rather, the superficial: good looks, talent, etc. Having a solid connection with one or two friends can be more fulfilling than being popular.

2. Be cognizant of your children's excessive desire to be sought after or crowd-pleasing. Talk to them about why they might consider it important. Provide examples of successful people who weren't necessarily "popular" as kids.

3. Do you know your child's friends personally and whether they're engaged in healthy activities? Keep tabs on who your children hang around with and what they do. Make sure they engage in healthy

ways of acting and communicating. Determine whether they've based their friendships on true bonding or on "false ground," such as the desire to be popular.

Establish an environment that will welcome and encourage your children's friends to hang out at your home. Invite the friends to the house and interact with them.

4. Do you know the parents of your child's friends? Communicate regularly with the parents of your children's friends. Give their parents a call and discuss relationships, curfew, homework, etc.

5. Does your child have a disability or other trait that makes him more vulnerable to social isolation? If so, be open to discussions. An important part of connecting to others is relating in an authentic fashion. This is not always easy, but children do better when we address their real concerns, fears, and joys. Be aware of social stigmas and communicate regularly with the child about how to handle them. Help him or her find ways to establish positive social relationships.

By listening to children, parents can get a sense of how their kids fit in with their social groups. Listen, but do not intrude. Children do better when left to fix their own problems; but parental advice is important.

Making Connection a Part of Everyday Life

Children who manage to establish healthy connections with others have an easier time in life than those who do not. Having good relationships—bonding and belonging—not only helps children function, but also serves as the basis for deepening their sense of connection to something larger. Try these activities to help your children deepen their connections with others.

If you have 3 minutes . . .

- Encourage your child to ask questions of others, even as simple as "How are you?" This gives other people the opportunity to share and connect with your child.

- Say, "I love you just because you're you!" Expressing unconditional love allows your child to feel secure enough to be herself.

- Remind your child about her good qualities and the importance of being true to self.

- Leave your child a note in her lunchbox or on her bedroom door expressing what you like about her.

- On rainy or snowy days, suggest to your child to pick up your neighbor's newspaper on their front lawn and personally deliver it.

- Show your child how to be a good listener, by listening.

- Encourage your child to smile and say "Hi" to a classmate she doesn't know.

If you have 30 minutes . . .

- Ask your child about her friends. Share your own experience about a friend or appreciated coworker you spent time with.

- Plan something you can do routinely as a family, like play a card or board game, work on crossword puzzles together, or cook a meal.

- Teach your child the art of communicating on paper: become pen pals with seniors or long-distance relatives, and send get-well cards to the sick. Your house of worship, school, or hospitals can provide a list.

- Read a story that has teasing or bullying as the theme. Use the opportunity to discuss the characters and their feelings.

- Go with your child to visit a neighbor and ask her personal questions about her life. Make note of her favorite book, movie, flower, and other interests and then bring that "special gift" to her on her birthday or holiday.

If you have 3 hours . . .

- Make a "goodie" basket for new neighbors, someone in the hospital, a family with a new baby, or a family in need—and deliver it together.

- Spend an afternoon at the park with another family. Ask the family of one of your child's classmates to meet up with your family.

- Prepare a picnic lunch together and go to a park. Eat leisurely. Take a long walk with your child. On some occasions, invite your child to bring a friend or two.

- Plan parties with a purpose. Perhaps a pajama party where friends work together to make no-sew blankets for foster children. Or encourage your child to ask friends to bring a book to donate, instead of a gift, to his next birthday party. Then you and your child can put the books together and deliver them to a school or child-care program.

- Partner with local Boys and Girls Club members and make flower boxes for Habitat for Humanity homes.

- Pick up kids from the homeless shelter and take them on a day's outing (bowling, zoo, museum, etc.).

If you have 3 days . . .

- Adopt an elderly or handicapped person in your area. Offer to mow her lawn, rake leaves, or shovel snow. Read a book or newspaper to your friend if she is visually impaired or ailing.

Learning compassion for animals

A Boys & Girls Club member enjoys time with her new senior friend.

Conversation Starters for Parents and Children

Sometimes it's difficult to get kids to open up about their friendships. Instead of drilling them about their friends or social situations, get them to think about the quality of their social connections by sharing these questions with them.

- How do you respond when kids are teasing an "outcast"?

- How do you feel about kids who are different from you?

- If you are teased, how does it make you feel?

- Is it possible that kids who don't fit in may actually have something in common with you? Can you give an example?

- Do you ever get angry at other kids, and what do you do about it?

- Do you think that kids are more violent these days? If yes, why do you think so?

- What do you think are ways to connect with other kids your age?

- How can we connect with other people in our neighborhood?

"Those who bring sunshine to the lives of others cannot keep it from themselves."

—Sir James Barrie

6

The Touchstone of Perspective

How Does Your Child See His Life and the World around Him?

"We don't see things as they are, we see them as we are."

—Anaïs Nin

When Nicole arrived at the First Presbyterian Church that Sunday afternoon, she felt terribly scared. Through her ten-year-old eyes, she watched a line of adults, children, and families forming around the building. Some had tattered clothes and pushed grocery carts, while others sang or chatted to each other. As she walked past them, she hovered next to her mom and siblings. They headed into the church for one single purpose: to feed the homeless.

After she entered the church and proceeded into the kitchen, Nicole's anxiety increased. She couldn't help but label the homeless people outside as "scary" and "dangerous." They didn't look like her, and they lived on the street. She had never interacted with a homeless person before, something she knew would happen that day. That frightened her. She was afraid of the unknown.

However, there wasn't much time to worry. In the kitchen, the group of Kids Korps volunteers had a lot of things to prepare before they opened the soup line and cafeteria. Nicole's family immediately started cleaning up the cafeteria for the guests and organizing the stands of condiments. Before the soup kitchen was ready to open, all volunteers assembled in the back of the kitchen to wash their hands and briefly discuss the events of the day.

The leader said, "Don't worry about any of the homeless guests, but be cautious."

That scared Nicole. He informed them about the importance of being as helpful and enthusiastic as possible, because it makes the whole experience much more rewarding. Then he paired the volunteers together and assigned everyone to stations. Nicole's job was to work at the drink station and pour drinks for each homeless guest.

She remembered wishing she could stay in the kitchen preparing trays or ladling soup. Those volunteers didn't really have to interact with the homeless as Nicole would. Her mom and siblings got to work in the kitchen . . . and Nicole would be out there with the homeless, feeling apprehensive and alone.

When the first guest arrived at her table, Nicole nervously asked him what he wanted to drink. As simple as this may seem, she felt vulnerable and unsure.

He replied with a smile, "Lemonade, please."

Nicole smiled back.

Slowly, but surely, she started to feel more relaxed around each person who passed by her drink table. Their gratitude to the volunteers was obvious. Almost everyone said "thank you," or expressed their appreciation with warm smiles. Nicole began to feel proud and fortunate to be there that afternoon helping people who were so desperate for a nice meal.

Nicole will never forget one particular little girl. After she had been serving drinks for about two hours, she noticed a small family getting into the soup line. They caught her eye for some reason, maybe because of their cute little daughter who couldn't have been any more than seven years old. Her blonde hair was pulled into a ponytail and she had a contagious smile. When she came over to Nicole's drink stand, she asked for lemonade, and Nicole poured her a glass. After Nicole handed her the lemonade, the girl still stood there, just looking at her.

Nicole realized the little blonde was staring at the candy necklace around Nicole's neck; she'd just bought it that same afternoon.

With longing eyes, the little girl said, "I used to have one of those."

Nicole instantly wanted to do something to make the girl's day special. She removed her candy necklace and placed it around the little girl's neck.

"I want you to have it," Nicole said.

The little girl's eyes lit up. She thanked Nicole and ran to show her mother.

Since that first experience at the soup kitchen, Nicole has volunteered at the First Presbyterian Church whenever she can. It is her favorite service project because it is so rewarding. Each time she helps a new homeless person at the soup kitchen, she sees that these people, whom she used to fear, are just people like herself. They aren't different; they just aren't as lucky as some people in this world.

Even today, she occasionally sees people at the soup kitchen whom she had helped years before, and when she does, she experiences a flood of strong emotions.

Although Nicole will probably never see that little blonde girl again, she knows she touched the girl's life in some small way—and also, that the little girl touched Nicole's in a very big way.

When we look past what we see, into what is actually there, our point of view does a quick shift. Certainly, we're not all required to see things the same way, but seeing a situation "correctly" or "for what it is" is often important, isn't it? Going beyond Nicky's enlightening experience, we can apply her change of perspective to many facets of life. Assessing a situation, for example, could be crucial. What if your child's safety and well-being depended on his accurate perspective of a happening? It may be important for our children to know how to assess a predicament correctly, or at least realize what they see may not be accurate. In fact, how many disagreements could we avoid with a child, spouse, or friend if we recognized the role that perspective plays in our lives? Healthy perspective helps our children consider different views through which they can arrive at a best conclusion, solution, or decision.

Of course, we can't always choose what experiences our children will encounter as they go about their daily lives, but we can teach our kids to examine their assumptions so they can better evaluate what they see. This can help them ask the right questions.

So, through what lens does your child see his life and the world around him? And why does it matter?

The Touchstone of Perspective

Perspective is about outlook, viewpoint, and perception—the lens through which we see the world around us, and even the circumstances of our own lives. While the familiar question "*Do you see the glass half full or half empty?*" typifies the role of optimism in affecting an outcome, it also makes the point of how we see things. Seeing life and circumstances through the lens of the half-full glass, for example, provides an added edge in experiencing happiness and contentment, and often lessens the blow of life's calamities.

Certainly, both positive and negative external events shape our lives in powerful ways—such as the birth of a baby or the loss of a loved one. But sometimes paradigm shifts in concepts don't come from an *outward* pivotal point, but an *internal* one, such as the realization that we've fallen in love. It's important to communicate to our kids how situations in life can change, and that we have choices in how to deal with those changes. These choices will influence how our kids will view their purpose in life.

So does it really matter how our children view life? Is it important, for example, whether they have a more negative or more positive perspective? The answer to both questions is "yes," and the reason: because how we *think* determines how we *act*. Actions stem from *what* and *how* we think.

Consider the following: Sitting on the bus one day, you notice when a woman and two teenage boys get aboard. The woman takes a seat, pulls a book out of her bag, and begins reading. Meanwhile, the two boys, who sat in separate seats a couple of rows behind her, take some sheets of paper from their backpacks and fold them into paper planes. Then they stand and toss them into the air, aiming at no one in particular. Five other onlookers take in the scene. Their thoughts:

Observer # 1: How can a mother be so unconcerned? How can she possibly have a boys-will-be-boys attitude about her sons' behavior on a public bus?

Observer # 2: What poor behavior! Those boys are old enough to know better.

Observer # 3: What a terrible bus driver! He's not taking any responsibility for keeping his passengers safe.

Observer # 4: Oh, that looks like so much fun! I hope the paper airplane sails over here so I can return it!

Observer # 5: That woman who got on the bus with those boys can't be their mother, because if she were, she'd ask them to sit down so they won't either get hurt or hurt others if the bus comes to a sudden stop.

These five onlookers, viewing the same event, had a different take on what they saw. But, more important than how each of them perceived the situation differently is the fact that each person will *act* according to his or her thoughts. Continuing with the example, let's say the five onlookers chose to act on their perceptions. Here's what might occur:

Onlooker # 1 says something to the mother: "Excuse me, ma'am. Are you aware that your boys are misbehaving?"

Onlooker # 2 says something to the boys themselves: "You guys need to sit down. If you don't, you might hurt yourselves or someone else."

Onlooker # 3 says something to the bus driver: "Excuse me, sir, but are you aware of the two boys in back who are disturbing others?"

Onlooker # 4 reaches up and grabs the nearest paper airplane and then sends it sailing through the air, thus keeping the game going.

Onlooker # 5 says to the person beside her: "I bet that woman who got on with those boys hopes the rest of us don't think those boys belong to her!"

Just as viewpoints of the same incident can vary greatly, they can also change with additional information. For instance, if the woman had suddenly stood up and told her sons to behave, Onlooker # 1 would no longer believe the mother ignored the kids' actions, and Onlooker # 5 would have realized an incorrect take on the situation.

We want to know how our children see things. Although we have some control over what our children do or don't do at home, once they go out the door, we don't always know what they will be exposed to and/or how it will shape or color the way they see things. Take, for example, our teen's view on using drugs. We may think we know his viewpoint on the issue, but do we really? We probably taught our child to "say no" to drugs, but will his saying "no" to friends last year mean "no" this year if he now encounters classmates or friends who use drugs? How can we know if the child will now wonder if using is okay as long as you don't get hooked, or even decide drugs are okay and join in? Knowing our children's take on this issue—and other issues—matters.

It may help to understand a child's developing brain. Teenage children's unpredictable moods, while anticipated, are somewhat of a mystery to most parents. Are our children just being contrary? Are they chemically altered? Or are they prisoner to their hormones? A recent scientific study shows there may be something to add to our questions about why adolescents behave the way they do.

With the aid of MRI (magnetic resonance imaging) technology, we can now see there is a wave of synapse formation in children just before puberty, around age eleven in girls and twelve in boys, and then there is an ebb in adolescence. Teens' prefrontal cortexes—responsible for planning, organization, and managing mood—recede and do not fully develop until age seventeen to nineteen.[1]

This suggests, for a period of time, our growing teens have a marginal "executive center." Until their neural pathways are reformed and laid down, what we expose our children to is important. Neuroscientist Jay Giedd describes the daily living consequences of this developmental phenomenon: "If a teen is doing music, sports, or academics, those are connections that will be hardwired in. If they're lying on the couch or playing video games or MTV, these are the cells and connections that are going to survive."[2]

So what does this mean? It means *we* can help wire in what becomes important to our kids. Kids Korps parents have discovered the truth in this as they involve their kids in community service and provide opportunities for them to meet and work side by side with positive people on meaningful activities. We have found that providing children with opportunities to care about others and to lend a helping hand helps create a philosophy of life: Caring about others makes a difference. When people support one another everyone benefits. The concept that caring for others will benefit everyone is something we can help "wire in."

So how do our children see the world? Do they view life through a lens that focuses on love and caring, or is it time to help our children acquire a new and improved way of seeing things?

Why Perspective Is a Good Thing for Your Child: Six Key Benefits

Teaching our children the importance of cleaning their "perception lens" has many positive implications for their mental and emotional development. Here are some of the reasons why we want to help our children clearly see and make decisions based on a bigger picture.

1. A positive perspective helps to mature children in healthy ways. When children create a balanced perspective, they tend to be less reactive in their decision-making. Equalizing their thoughts or approach restrains children's natural inclination toward impulsivity, which often brings negative results. As children develop the skills to look, evaluate, and then decide, they gain the maturity to evaluate their options more clearly and handle situations with greater equanimity—calmly, even in the face of challenges. By helping our children develop a positive perspective, we help them to use wisdom in their approach to life. Often, our child's well-being depends on the ability to make a sound decision or a good choice. But if he operates from incorrect information or a biased assumption, will he arrive at the best conclusions and therefore find the best solution? For example, your child says, "I cheated on the test because everyone at school does, and no one feels it's a bad thing to do." If you help your child see that cheating is wrong and that it can negatively affect the grading curve and hurt other students—then your child will have a different perspective on cheating, regardless of what his friends do, and be inclined to take responsibility for his own actions.

2. A sensible perspective encourages greater acceptance and tolerance of others. A healthy perspective helps children value diversity. Not everyone looks at life, acts, or sees things just the way we do. Helping our children develop the ability to adapt to their surroundings and others' needs will open doors to understanding and love. Conversely, a clouded or selfish perspective can result in a lack of sensitivity toward others, leaving children feeling frustrated, rejected, and isolated. Children who operate from a perspective focused solely on themselves will likely suffer the consequences of not having an abundance of close and caring friendships. People who show acceptance and the willingness to entertain different ideas, views, and possibilities draw others to them. When a child sees through a more expansive lens, possibilities open up and a greater tolerance develops. One Kids Korps volunteer, fifteen-year-old Lindsay, expressed her understanding so well: "We came from different backgrounds and ethnic groups, yet there was nothing that separated us as people when I was with those kids."

3. A healthy perspective helps children become aware of, and accept, their authentic selves. A good perspective allows children to see not just others and the world around them more clearly, but also themselves. They more easily, and usually more willingly, learn to accept themselves and their limitations. When children learn to live with their own strengths and weaknesses, they can develop their strong points and modify what doesn't work for them. Feeling secure in their own individual make-up also gives them greater ability to know that while they can learn much from their successes, they can also strengthen their character through their mistakes and failures. And children who feel capable of "thinking things through," of examining things before making decisions, will less likely follow others aimlessly. Children will more likely stand *for* something they believe in—and *against* what they don't—rather than follow the pack. They are being true to themselves.

4. An objective perspective gives children a sense of being in charge. We can't always change our circumstances, but we can control how we respond to them. An otherwise devastating slight by a friend will not have as negative an impact on our kids if they have a positive perspective and feel they can manage their feelings. When we have the ability to assess a situation accurately, and when we feel we can affect some control over our own lives by choosing how we will react, it is empowering. An objective perspective helps children learn to prepare for whatever comes their way.

5. An understanding perspective cultivates compassion for others. Children with a mature perspective on life will more likely empathize with people going through hard times. They understand and see the need for help, not criticism. Knowing how a variety of factors cause people's difficult situations can help children feel more compassionate. A sound perspective helps children to walk in someone else's shoes.

6. A sound perspective develops optimism. When children see life and circumstance from the mindset of having a half-full glass (versus half empty), they won't unduly magnify the problems of life or allow guilt, blame, and shame to paralyze them. They can handle frustration more successfully and see setbacks not as failures, but as opportunities for growth and wisdom. Anticipating a light at the end of the tunnel or another avenue to follow can help children persevere and keep them from magnifying their problems and focusing on the negative.

Making blankets for homeless and abused children brings friends together.

Kids who have the ability to see things with expanded vision, or through others' eyes, are more compassionate and understanding toward those around them. As young children, they're less likely to bully and belittle others "different" from themselves. As they grow, they will more likely respond to the needs of others and prioritize their own needs and desires in balanced and healthy ways. Gaining perspective of the world around them and having the maturity to think and act with equanimity not only gives our children a better sense of purpose in their own lives, but also allows them to work as stewards to their peers in setting good examples and fostering a caring and nurturing environment.

Helping Children "Get" the Lesson: The "Aha Shift"

On their drive home, Nicole told her mom about giving the little girl her necklace. Nicole said, "You know, Mom, just because they're homeless doesn't mean they've always lived that way. In fact, that little girl used to have a candy necklace just like mine."

Her mom smiled and said, "You're right, Nicole. People are homeless for a variety of reasons. They may not be homeless forever but when they are, that's when they need our help the most. I'm really proud of you for seeing our day through that little girl's eyes."

Because Nicole's mom believed in helping others, she gave Nicole the opportunity to learn about people in different circumstances.

Giving your children the opportunity to see things from another point of view gives them perspective. By engaging your kids in a variety of experiences, they become more open-minded and less judgmental.

"When you change the way you look at things, the things you look at change."

—Dr. Wayne W. Dyer

Eight Ways to Help Your Children Gain Perspective

The benefits of a healthy perspective give us a good idea of the importance of making an impact on our child's take on the world. Following are some things we can do to help our children grow in their ability to form a positive view of the world:

1. Examine your own paradigm. A perspective paradigm serves as a model or pattern for behavior. What kind of life view are we modeling for our children? How do we see our own world? For example: Do we consider it self-indulgent to take time out for ourselves, something for which we rarely have time? Or, do we see it as a necessity—in order to rest, reflect, and restore ourselves—a responsibility we have to self, family, and others?

Is being assertive an opportunity for us to communicate openly, clearly, and directly with others? Or do we see assertiveness as a negative trait?

When we help our children learn the value of perspective, we help them learn to question. Questioning helps them understand that a "positive view" is a choice they can make. Our own healthy paradigm can guide our children.

2. Watch for opportunities to teach your children the importance of examining their view of things. Look for "teachable moments" and assist your children in gaining a broader scope on things. Engage them in a discussion about what they see and how they came to their conclusions. If your child witnesses, for example, a child being teased, first ask him to relate the experience as he saw it—through his *own* eyes. Then have him explain the situation through the eyes of the child who received the taunting. Watch how the story changes. In this way, he will learn that the same situation can be viewed in different ways.

3. Talk with your children about seeing the other side of the coin. Teach your children that, more often than not, there are two sides to a story. At times, instead of a wrong or right option, they may recognize different choices. Help your children to put themselves in the other person's position, or see the bigger picture, before forming a conclusion.

4. Encourage your children to be possibility-thinkers. Kids who see every negative occurrence as the end of the world experience frustration and a sense of hopelessness about the future. Help your children see that a setback is just a setback, and something from which they can learn. Provide them with examples from your own life when a negative turned into a positive. Perhaps you didn't get accepted to the college of your choice, but it turned out that the school you did attend had a curriculum better suited for you and led to a career that you enjoy. Teach your children the meaning of the phrase, "When one door closes, another one opens."

5. Empower your children to believe they can affect the outcome. Let children know they *do* have a choice in how they view and handle circumstances. Teach them to ask themselves questions such as: *Compared to all of the things that have happened, are happening, or could happen in my life, how bad is this? How will this change my life tomorrow, next week, or next year? Is there some way I can use this experience in a positive way?* Perspective can help children see feelings for what they are, and help them understand how feelings change.

6. Provide opportunities for community service. Encourage your children to take an interest in charitable endeavors.

Participating in the community alongside people they might not otherwise meet broadens their perspective.

- If you take them to feed the homeless, they will gain insight into other people's circumstances.

- If they spend time in a senior center, they will hone in on elders' perspectives. In addition, tales of "the good old days" will probably make them appreciate the present-day conveniences.

Participating in community service offers your children experiences that will encourage them in developing perspective. You might want to make lists of participatory opportunities that can shape their perspective and influence them to become caring persons. Explain the importance of getting involved with community affairs.

7. Model good listening for your children. It's one thing to *hear* someone talking to you; it's another to really *listen*. Helping kids develop the skill of listening can shape perspective, because children, or any of us for that matter, are more likely to develop empathy and the skills of critical thinking when we really tap into others' words. Critical thinking comes to good listeners. They tend to evaluate a larger picture, which, in turn, helps them gain greater tolerance for others—an important step toward growing into caring and compassionate people.

8. Listen to your children's perspective. It's important to listen what they have to say because our attentiveness encourages them to value what they think. This deepens their search for the meaning of things.

If we encourage our children to discuss their perspective openly and analyze objectively the situations they see and encounter—and let them know we are truly listening—they are bound to embrace wiser, more mature views of these issues.

How Does Your Child See the World?

1. Your child tries out for the school play, but the role goes to someone else. Your child is likely to say:
   a. "I knew I wasn't going to get selected. I'm just no good."
   b. "The director doesn't like me. He only picks his favorites."
   c. "The role went to someone else, so I'll try again for the next school play."

2. In the classroom, your child notices a student in front of him cheating. He says:
   a. "It's not my business. I'll just ignore it."
   b. "I think it's okay to cheat as long as you don't get caught."
   c. "I'm going to talk to the cheater after class. Maybe he doesn't understand that what he did matters to all of us."

3. Your family has an opportunity to spend the weekend helping to build a new house for a family in need. Your child says:
   a. "I don't want to go unless my friends come along."
   b. "The government is supposed to help them; why do we have to?"
   c. "I think it's important to help others."

4. Your child's classmate has a difficult time getting good grades in school. Your child says:
   a. "He's stupid."
   b. "His parents probably don't make him do his homework."
   c. "Maybe I'll ask him if he would like me to study with him sometime."

Think about the answers you chose and keep them in mind as you help mold your child's perspective.

Making Perspective a Part of Everyday Life

As with any skill, children need guidance to understand perspective. Here are some ways to lead.

Like her mom, my two-year-old granddaughter, Kendahl, is not a morning person. She is downright grumpy in the mornings. I chose not to accept that kind of disposition during those times when she stayed at Grandma's, and decided to set a tone of morning joy. When I heard her wake up, I went to her room and greeted her with a cheerful good morning. Then, picking her up, I sang and twirled her around as we made our way to the kitchen. There, we said good morning to the cat, the fish, and the flowers. Looking out the window, I chimed, "Good morning, world!"

When I first started doing this, she looked at me like I was a crazy woman, but that soon changed to an expression of laughter, and now she, too, participates. When she sees me enter her room, she starts singing and twirling even before we get to the kitchen. She looks for the cat so she can begin the hellos. In short, joy and happiness now fill her mornings. I've changed her perspective about how to "see" the world as she begins each day.

—Arlene Burres, grandparent

If you have 3 minutes . . .

- Fill dinner glasses half full and ask them if their glass is half full or half empty and why they chose their answer. Discuss the half full/half empty philosophy with them.

- Tell your children that every three seconds a child somewhere in the world dies from hunger or disease because of poverty. Get out a timer and have them calculate how many kids die in three minutes (Answer: 180 seconds divided by 3 seconds = 60 children).

- When you see someone who looks like he is from a different culture, ask your child where you think he is from and what might be unique about him.

- Blindfold your kids and have them walk around a room. Hold their arm and ask them what it feels like to be blind.

- Open a magazine and have your children pick out a picture. Each of you look at the picture and tell each other what you see.

If you have 30 minutes . . .

- Encourage your child to spend time with someone different from him: a younger or older child, an adult or elderly person, someone who will share a different point of view.

- As a family, collect toys and clothing and take them to people who are poor or needy; talk with your child about why some people might have gotten into dire straights.

- Watch the news and discuss the culture of another country; examine and discuss both the different attitudes and beliefs, and the similarities to your own.

If you have 3 hours . . .

- Help cook and/or serve a meal at a homeless shelter. Encourage your child to interact with the men, women, and children rather than hiding out somewhere.

- Take a family drive around other neighborhoods in your town so your kids can get a better understanding of the varying lifestyles.

- Take pictures of the people in your community as they play in parks, hang out in malls, or walk around town. Create a photo scrapbook called "Our Town."

- Arrange for you and your child to "shadow" a police officer, teacher, or firefighter to see what their daily work is like.

- Visit a cultural center that highlights the achievements of a different ethnic group.

- Choose a movie—perhaps an interesting documentary— that inspires a lot of deep thinking, and watch it with your children. Afterwards, discuss various perspectives about it.

If you have 3 days . . .

- Collect items for international relief; initiate a discussion with your child about the differences between people in our country and citizens of another country.

- Host a foreign-exchange student to see how she interprets our society through her eyes.

- Organize a "Stuff-a-Bag" Project. Collect toiletries, teddy bears, journals, and blankets to put in duffel bags and personally give to abused children living in residential treatment centers.

Stuffing duffel bags with blankets, teddy bears, and toiletries for abused and homeless children

Conversation Starters for Parents and Children

- If another child struggles in school, does that mean he's stupid or lazy, or could there be another explanation?

- Why do you think other families have different holiday traditions?

- Why do you think people in the world sometimes have trouble getting along?

- What can we do to make our community a better place to live?

- If you had one wish to make this country/world a better place, what would your wish be?

- Is there someone "different" at your school who's often taunted or ignored? Do you think that's right? Is there something you can do to change it?

- If you didn't get elected student president even though you thought you're the best person for the job, how would you react? Would it get you down, or would you be thinking about ways to improve your next campaign? Is there a way this situation might actually be a positive event?

- Has anyone ever made fun of you for being "different"? Do you feel pressure to be like everyone else? How does this make you feel?

"Get out there and do it. Where there's a will, there's a way, and if your heart is really into something, you can always make it work. There's nothing worse than sitting back and doing nothing, so take the first step. Each step that follows will get easier. Believe in yourself even if it seems nobody else does, and believe in your cause."

—Lindsay Logsdon, founder (at 15), Youth for a Better World in Canada

7

The Touchstone of Gratitude

Instilling the All-Important "Attitude of Gratitude" in Your Child

*"Gratitude is not only the greatest of virtues,
but the parent of all the others."*

—Cicero

Kevin had a rocky start in life. Weighing a mere two pounds at birth, he was hooked up to every monitor and tube imaginable, and spent the first six months of his life in the Neonatal Intensive Care Unit. Through numerous setbacks, surgeries, and close calls, little Kevin was a fighter. Slowly but steadily, his condition improved, and the day finally arrived when he could go home from the hospital. But the challenges didn't end there. Kevin's still-fragile health made him susceptible to many ills; two bouts with pneumonia in his delicate lungs almost took his life.

As years passed, Kevin grew healthier and healthier. But his parents never forgot how they'd almost lost him, and they showered him— their only child—with all that he desired. They filled Kevin's room with the latest toys and gadgets, most of which sat untouched in his closet or under his bed. Of course, Kevin's parents worried from time to time about spoiling him, but brushed their fears aside—until it all came to a head.

One day, Kevin—at age ten—sat looking through a car magazine with a friend. His mother overheard her son say, "Which do you think I should get when I have my license—a Mustang or a Corvette?"

"What makes you think you're going to get either of those?" his friend asked.

"My parents will get me anything I want!" Kevin bragged.

Kevin's mother turned away from the doorway, thinking: *time for a few changes around our household . . .*

The Touchstone of Gratitude

At times, after giving gifts to our kids, haven't most of us felt a tinge of irritation when they acted as if they did not appreciate our efforts and generosity? And even if they offered a half-hearted thank you, we didn't sense a genuine appreciation. Saying thank you, of course, expresses gratitude, but truly grateful people go beyond the display of good manners when they *show* thankfulness. A television program recently featured a boy opening a present and, when he saw the contents, he sprang up, yelling, "Yes, yes, yes!" He twirled around, jumped up and down, twirled again, and raised both arms in the air—as though he had just won a race. Whether or not this boy felt gratitude deep in his heart is hard to determine, but his enthusiasm for what he had received certainly created an environment of joy!

Gratitude *can* create joy. Gratitude is an attitude—a *positive* attitude about daily pleasures, ordinary events, even the essentials we take for granted, like our next breath. A sense of gratitude helps children learn to be happy in the moment and appreciate what they have.

Although the process of helping kids develop an attitude of gratitude takes a mindful and ongoing dedication, the rewards last a lifetime. Many of us walk through life using a "deferred payment plan." How often do we catch ourselves thinking, "I'll be happy when . . ."? Difficult to admit, but so true. Instead, we must model appreciation and the happy results. If we don't show our gratefulness, how can we expect our kids to?

Today's "gimme" culture leads too many of our children further and further away from experiencing gratitude. And we know by now that having more doesn't guarantee happiness. Articles have spouted: "There are more suicides on Wall Street than in the ghetto"—a sad comment on the "if I get it, I'll be happy" theory. Being grateful for the blessings we enjoy *right now,* instead of waiting for some other day to find happiness, comes to our kids through positive interchange.

Christina, a ten-year-old girl whose mother involved her in community service at age six, reflected on her experience as a volunteer. She understands the importance of integrating gratefulness into her life: She told us how, through her volunteer experiences, she's learned thankfulness in regard to what she has, every day of her life. Christine feels empathy for the people she has met. Some have no house, no food, no parents, and no money and all live very hard lives.

Helping our kids develop an attitude of gratitude doesn't happen overnight. It takes considerable patience, understanding, and, most important, setting the example. We want our children to learn that gratitude goes further than thanking Aunt Martha for the socks she sent them for Christmas. We want our children to discover and understand that cultivating gratitude can lead them to joy in all situations. Gratitude, we want our kids to learn, grows from planting healthy seeds of thankfulness into each day. When we do this, gratitude crops up continually and becomes a way of life.

Children will develop healthy attitudes at their own pace. Try to keep your child steeped in opportunities to care for family, friends, community, and themselves. The constant pruning by parents creates a sturdy child. Teaching children not just to *say* thanks, but also to *feel* thanks leads them to experience the benefits that come from living a grateful life. We can help them feel this thanks by bringing their attention to moments of joy in their lives, and in ours. When fourteen-year-old Katie finished her fourth service project, she announced: "It never ceases to amaze me what people can do when working together to achieve a goal. I am so thankful to be part of this team!"

"Let us be grateful to people who make us happy; they are the charming gardeners who make our souls blossom."

—Marcel Proust

Why Gratitude Is a Good Thing for Your Child: Six Key Benefits

Teaching children not just to *say* thank you, but showing them ways to *feel* thanks, leads them to experience the benefits that come from living a grateful life, such as:

1. Hopefulness and optimism. When people feel genuinely grateful, their appreciation rubs off onto others and nourishes connections. Being rooted in and surrounded by positive relationships promotes the likelihood of our children embracing a positive outlook on life. And when they feel more hopeful and confident, they are better prepared to tackle difficulties. All children feel overwhelmed when confronted with problems—especially as teenagers. Rocky Balboa told his son, "Life can knock you to your knees sometimes."

Having perspective helps our kids get back up, and knowing they have a choice can breed gratitude. Children's end-of-the-world response to ordeals is softened significantly by gratefulness. A grateful heart can help children look for the silver lining in a challenging situation. Children who learn gratitude can see myriad opportunities. Gratefulness and optimism go hand in hand and diminish feelings of negativity. Manny Diotte, a motivational speaker and writer (*Happiness Is a Pair of Shorts*), is a walking miracle. He developed Hodgkin's disease as a child and overcame the cancer. Manny believes the best time to be happy is between yesterday and tomorrow. He'll be the first to tell you grateful living has many benefits and he learned this lesson as a child.

2. Better health. A thankful heart is good medicine. According to research by Dr. Michael McCullough: Those who describe themselves as grateful to others, or to a higher power, tend to be more optimistic, have a higher level of vitality, and suffer less from stress and depression.[1] Being thankful literally changes our hormones, increases our blood flow, and can give our cells more oxygen. An attitude of gratitude can help us live not just happier, but also longer lives.[2]

3. Greater generosity. Have you noticed that when a child shows gratitude, he often brings generosity to others? We've seen kids visit children who live in foster-care shelters and come away grateful to simply have parents, to eat dinner together, or to have their own room. So often kids feel that everything revolves around them, but when they realize many other children don't share that security, they learn to appreciate what's often taken for granted and to interact with a more generous heart. Gratefulness and selfishness can't really coexist, and how exciting it is when our children think beyond their own personal needs—when they direct their actions toward giving to others, rather than getting something for themselves.

4. Spontaneous joy and reciprocity. When our children are grateful, joy comes more easily and more spontaneously, and they often pass it on. A study published in 2006 showed that when subjects felt appreciation for someone who helped them, they were more likely to reciprocate not only with the person who helped them, but also with strangers.[3] The action of doing good deeds can consciously and sincerely pass on from one person to another, resulting in the effects spreading like ripples in a pond.

5. Thoughtfulness and vision. Sometimes it takes a little extra nudge to show our kids that giving of themselves can feel good. Only through experience—through doing—can they begin to recognize that certain goals may require giving something up in order to gain something that matters more. Developing this ability to sacrifice or delay gratification for a larger goal or a greater good is a character-building, lifelong asset.

6. Higher priorities. Kids with a developed sense of appreciation and gratitude are more inclined to prioritize what is important in life. Spending time with family, acknowledging others' feelings, and showing kindness to people become as, or more, important to them as getting the latest style of jeans or getting the newest iPod. An internal spirit of gratitude does not depend on external rewards such as peer status, possessions, or even accomplishments. Of course, teens naturally find fashion and celebrities important, but gratitude simply helps elevate what *is* most important to the top position. Teaching our children to appreciate the everyday things helps to ground them. Feeling grateful for what they have can ward off feelings of inadequacy even if they don't have the coolest (and most expensive) sneakers or the new video game system. Their self-worth will not depend on acquiring more. Research shows that grateful people put less importance on material goods. They are less likely to judge their own success in terms of possessions, less envious of wealthy persons, and more inclined to share what they have.[4]

Jarred, age eight, resented having to go to an orphanage and the giving up of one of his toys to bring to a child. At age eight, giving up a toy certainly was not on his agenda. Finally, after searching through the garage for some old toys, he found a plastic rolling golf cart—once his favorite, until all the golf clubs and balls had disappeared. He thought, "Perfect. I never will use this again anyway." When he arrived at the orphanage, seventy anxious orphans eagerly waited for the toy they would receive from their new friends. Before they'd finished unloading the toys, a little five-year-old boy ran to get his first choice: Jarred's golf cart. This surprised Jarred and made him feel proud to have his toy chosen first. Something that meant nothing to him was special to another kid. Jarred watched the little boy hold onto that golf cart the entire day. On the way home from the orphanage, Jarred spoke little and seemed to be in deep thought.

When he arrived home that evening, Jarred started searching for the missing golf balls and golf clubs. When he found them he said, "Mom, can we go back to the orphanage to give these to my friend?"

Often, children cannot change their circumstances, but they can find meaning and purpose *within* their struggles, large or small, through gratitude.

What a wonderful way to teach our children to give to others! We shopped together, and my children picked out the gifts they wanted a six-year-old and eight-year-old girl to receive. The first time my son and daughter brought holiday presents to these kids who had suffered abuse, they experienced the joy of giving . They loved seeing the kids' joyful expressions when opening their gifts, and they didn't expect anything in return.

—Karen, parent

Helping Children "Get" the Lesson:
The "Aha Shift"

In the story at the beginning of this chapter, Kevin's attitude definitely needed repair. Kevin's parents hadn't realized until after he'd turned ten what a disservice they had done to him by catering to his every whim. After all, they loved seeing the joy in their son's eyes when he received another gift from them. But after his mother overheard the startling conversation between Kevin and his friend, she and her husband sat down and ironed out a new strategy for raising their son to *care*.

Kevin's parents went into his room the next day with three large boxes. They labeled boxes: Trash, Charity, and Resale. They told him, "We're going to go through everything in your room to determine if it's getting used or just taking up space. If you're not using it, we then decide which box it goes into." Kevin resisted this new plan, not so much because he minded giving stuff away—after all, he had so much—but because he didn't want to spend his free time sorting his things. But, his parents remained firm, and they spent the next week with Kevin giving his room a thorough going-through. Eventually, Kevin earned almost $500 selling his stuff on eBay, and his parents again took a stand about how he would spend it. "One-third is yours to keep, one-third goes into a savings account, and we'll donate the final third to a charity of your choice."

They also started volunteering as a family. By the time Kevin started high school, he'd made a subtle shift in his priorities and an even more important change in his personality. He felt good when he served food to homeless people, he liked visiting with orphaned children, and all the stuff he had long ago taken pride in, while still important, had less priority in his life. Kevin learned firsthand that not every kid has a new video game system—or even a bed to sleep in!

Kevin's sixteenth birthday passed without a car sitting in the driveway, and Kevin didn't seem to notice. Two years later, during his senior year, the school staff held an end-of-the-year awards assembly to recognize students who stood out because of their exceptional performance in sports, academics, or extracurricular activities. They awarded the Best

Citizenship Award, which goes to the person who contributed the most in a positive and significant way to the school, to Kevin—a football player, student body vice president, and president of Youth for a Better Tomorrow. He'd come so far but, in an illustration of the depth and genuineness of his gratitude, Kevin surprised the entire audience that night—and one deserving man in particular—with an announcement of his own.

Kevin leaped on stage, eyes shining with enthusiasm, and thanked the audience sincerely for the honor. "But," he raised his voice above the applause to explain, "there's someone who deserves this as much as I do." The crowd grew silent at his unexpected words. "Someone who spends more hours at this school than any of us. Someone who gets here before we do, and who's here long after we're gone. Someone who we see picking up a carelessly discarded candy wrapper or soda can. Someone who has attended just about every special event, every football, baseball, basketball, softball, and soccer game this school has held. You name it, he's there, cheering us on, cleaning up before and after, and taking pride in everything about this school.

"I've seen him out in the parking lot helping a student change a tire, walking students to the nurse's office when they didn't feel well, or just listening when someone needed to talk, and offering words of encouragement. Joking with students, searching a trash can for a lost assignment, even lending a shoulder to cry on . . . he's done everything for us, and I've never seen him get the credit he deserves—or *any* credit, for that matter. Not that he'd ever ask for any. For him, it's an honor just to do his job. So tonight, I'd like to see this award go, instead, to Mr. Paul."

Rising to their feet, the audience went wild, chanting, "Mr. Paul! Mr. Paul! Mr. Paul!" Mr. Paul, the school's tireless and dedicated custodian, looked a little embarrassed and overwhelmed, but he beamed as many students coaxed him to get up on stage and accept his award. For years, Mr. Paul had served students with gratitude simply for the opportunity. With tears in his eyes, Mr. Paul said, "Thank you so much. I don't know what to say, other than I've only accomplished two important things in my whole life—first, successfully serving this fine school in a job I've loved and, second, having you share this award with me, because it makes me realize that you know I love you all as much as I do."

Nobody wiped more tears from their eyes than Kevin's parents. Kevin had learned the lesson about gratitude and was teaching it to the entire school.

Four Ways to Help Children Experience and Express Gratitude

As we saw in Kevin's story, learning gratitude is an acquired trait—something learned over a period of time through exposure to experiences that inspire a spirit of gratitude. Some tips for ensuring that your kids will take part in these types of experiences and learn from them:

1. Show, don't tell. What can we do to show our appreciation of and toward others? Do you stop and let your kids see you smile when something touches your heart? For example: your appreciation for a kind word, a sunset, a small child sharing candy with her brother. Do they see us help someone in need? In the process of teaching our kids to care, they learn more about who they are. We can remind our children, through our body language (as well as words), to show thanks whenever the opportunity presents itself. This sets up a simple expectation to appreciate what others do for us. Although saying "Thank you" has merit, *showing* their thanks through actions hits home.

2. Create a special "appreciation location." Designate a place in your house—a bulletin board, the refrigerator, a shelf, or a table—to showcase items that will substantiate your pleasure and thoroughly make your children feel appreciated. In addition, the display will acknowledge their appreciation for others. Items might include:

- pictures they have created and take pleasure in

- special photos

- greeting cards

- gifts they've made for a parent

- a letter from Grandma or Grandpa that made them feel good

Use anything that not only helps them feel grateful, but also prompts talks about being thankful.

3. Encourage your children to think good thoughts and act on them. Talk with your children about how people sometimes have bad days, go through bad moods as they struggle with something, or don't have good thoughts. Then explain that thoughts and words can make a difference. We can encourage our children to think good thoughts the next time we run into a grouchy checkout clerk. Decide on a secret cue (a wink or a little touch). Kids love secrets! Thinking good thoughts and smiling translate into a contagious positive attitude. The results may surprise you. The person may even smile back! At the very least, you and your children will feel an internal boost by sharing this positive little secret and a grateful attitude. Have you noticed how so many people look down or away as they pass you in a mall, on the street, or in a store? Try an experiment. Smile at the person when you and your children pass someone. If you can, say hello. Your children will be surprised at the number of people who smile or say "Hi" in return.

4. Help your child find the positive in the negative. One of the best lessons we instill in our children comes through looking for either the good, or a solid

Making heart-shaped footstools for seniors

Gratitude is a two-way street—a young orphan and teen enjoy one another's company

message, in the challenging situations of life. If we remind them to be grateful for what they have, they may see the situation from a different perspective. When we encounter a setback in our own life, we have the opportunity to show how gratefulness puts things into perspective.

Three Levels of Gratitude

It helps to clarify the ways our children can experience, and express, their gratitude. We have identified three levels of gratitude. Before we can ask children to own their feelings of thanks, we must first understand which level they're on, and focus accordingly.

1. Being thankful for what is done for us. Generally, we find it easy to express gratitude when someone has done something kind for us. Even then, however, some more negatively inclined children, or children simply in a bad mood, can find it hard to say thank you or show their appreciation. Teaching them to look others in the eye and say thank you, or to write a thank-you note when they've received a gift, encourages simple thanks for a kind gesture or deed.

> "Every single person you meet has an imaginary sign around his or her neck that says, "Make me feel important." If you can do that, you'll be a success not only in business, but in life as well."
>
> —Mary Kay Ash, founder, Mary Kay Cosmetics

2. Being thankful for what we have. This next level can pose more of a challenge, for sometimes we find it more difficult to stop and recognize the good things in our lives that we usually take for granted. Children don't often give much attention to food, shelter, ease of living, and love of family. As parents, we may think we can't get them to appreciate the meeting of their basic needs—but we can. In fact, it is our *responsibility*. You may discover, as you witness your child becoming more fulfilled, that it is also our *pleasure*.

3. **Finding something to be thankful for, despite the bad.** The third level of gratitude is the ability to find good even when many would consider the situation doesn't warrant it. While it is hard for children and teens to find something to appreciate about a missed goal, or their first fender bender, they can focus on the lesson: "If I practice, I will do better," or "I realize how easy it is to make a mistake, and I'm more aware now. I'm a safer driver."

When they find they feel gratitude even if they feel bad, they will experience the satisfaction that comes from knowing how problems don't have the power to bully or keep them down—and that perhaps they even have a solution. This will make them want to find the good in the bad more often. It's a self-perpetuating lesson.

How Kevin's Parents Made a Difference

Kevin thought his parents would give him anything, even an expensive car. Fortunately, Kevin's parents recognized the signs of overindulgence and selfishness in their son and knew they must rebuild his character. Not only did they talk with their son about ways in which he could share the wealth, but they also showed, through their own actions, that practicing gratitude is a way of life. Kevin's family started taking him into the community to *experience* situations where people had little, but still felt fortunate. When his parents stopped their overindulgence, Kevin learned to give back, and when they helped him experience life through the eyes of others who had less, Kevin grew to feel grateful and not take what he had for granted. He had to balance what he wanted with the needs of others in his community. His family gradually and continuously made gratitude a way of life, and it paid off for their family. Their point: we all can shift our focus and make positive changes in our own homes. We can teach our kids, "We are a family that marks our blessings." Not only will they develop into better people with this new attitude, but we will, too.

Is Your Child Living a Thankful Life?

Many of us remember the times our parents said, "Eat everything on your plate. Kids are starving in Africa!" To be honest, most of us had no clue about the lives of African children. Most of our parents went no further than this simple statement, and we certainly didn't feel grateful for the uneaten peas on our plate. Yuck! But today's media and technology bring us up close to the lives of children around the world, and our children can learn they have more than most other kids—much more. Our parents were right: We do need to give thanks, and we have myriad ways to do it. Let's take a look at how grateful *your* kids are:

1. Your teenager really wants a car for Christmas, but it's just not in your budget. When he's through opening his gifts and there's no car in sight, does he:
   a. Stomp out of the room in anger that he didn't get the car?
   b. Express disappointment and show sarcasm: "Couldn't bend for me, huh?"
   c. Smile in appreciation for his gifts and join the family for dinner?

2. You're walking out of the house with your daughter when you notice a beautiful sunset and point it out to her. Does she:
   a. Mumble and keep her eyes on the ground?
   b. Briefly glance at the sunset and say, "Yeah, it's nice"?
   c. Stop and appreciate the beautiful sight with you, even offer to get a camera?

3. Your son forgets to bring his science fair project to class, so you drive it to school for him. Does he:
   a. Grab it from you and run back to class?
   b. Grumble, "I can do this on my own, Mom!" and give you a dirty look?
   c. Express gratitude that you made yourself late for work in order to get his project to him?

4. Someone your child doesn't know gives him a compliment. Does he:
   a. Deny the compliment by insisting the speaker is wrong?
   b. Look down and mumble something like, "It's no big deal"?
   c. Look at the person, smile, and thank that person for the recognition?

5. You arrange to take your daughter to a homeless shelter to visit with the kids for a few hours. Does she:
   a. Get to the shelter and barely interact with the kids?
   b. Complain about going, but engage with the children once she's there, yet on the way home still pout about being made to go?
   c. Engage with the kids and on the trip home reflect with you about her own good fortune in life?

Making Gratitude a Part of Everyday Life

We would all love our children to *inwardly* feel the warmth that comes from a grateful spirit. When these feelings focus *toward* others, they tend to create good feelings inside us, as well. The time you take to show your child how to show gratitude is time well spent.

If you have 3 minutes . . .

- Practice a "30 seconds of gratitude" exercise. Help your child give thanks for something—a sunset, a family member, or a nice deed done.

- Encourage your child to pay a compliment to a loved one or to voice something he appreciates about that person.

- Ask your child to tell you something she likes about herself.

- Fill a "Gratitude Bowl" with short quotes, saying things such as "I feel grateful that my brother fixed my bike," "I feel

grateful that Mom took extra time to make this special dinner for us," or, "Today, I felt grateful for having strong legs to
walk to school." Then pass the bowl around the dinner table.
Family members can take turns reading a "gratitude quote"
or statement selected from the bowl.

If you have 30 minutes . . .

- "Touch the Earth" with your child. Spend some quiet
  time taking in the outdoors and appreciating nature.

- Encourage your child to write thank-you notes. Reflect on
  or send thanks for a gift or simple kindness, or to the host
  of a party or sleepover attended. Thank-you notes are a
  sign of good manners, a way for children to learn they
  reap what they sow, and a way for them to generate an
  ongoing attitude of gratitude.

- Take your child to the bank to open a savings account.
  Talk to her about giving a portion of the savings to a
  charity at the end of the year.

- Together, choose a "Just because I love you" card, and
  send it to someone special.

- Encourage your child to call a relative—aunt, uncle,
  grandparent—or a friend every weekend.

If you have 3 hours . . .

- Make a "gratitude visit" with your child. First, assist your
  child in writing a detailed "gratitude letter" to someone,
  explaining specifically how she appreciates that person.
  Then take the letter on the visit and read it out loud to
  the person.

- Help your child choose items from her closet to give away or sell, with a portion of the profits going to her favorite charity.

- Put together a care package to send to men in service and include a "gratitude" letter to thank them for their tremendous sacrifice and bravery.

- After your child chooses a book or toy of his own to give away, go together to give it to the Ronald McDonald House for siblings of sick kids.

If you have 3 days . . .

- Encourage your child to keep a gratitude journal. Starting at an early age, many kids like to keep track of the events in their lives. You can encourage your young child or teen to keep a journal of what he or she is thankful for. In her book *Simple Abundance,* Sarah Ban Breathnach suggests this is one of the best ways to build a "gratitude muscle."

Conversation Starters for Parents and Children

Talk with your children on a regular basis about gratitude and caring for others. Some questions to help you get started on a meaningful dialogue with your child:

- What and who in your life are you truly grateful for? Why? What makes these people or things so special?

- Do you feel you take some things for granted that perhaps you shouldn't? What would they be? What if you lived in different circumstances, like your house didn't have a bathroom? What if you didn't have food every day?

- If you could make yourself more aware of the many blessings you have (like good health, a good mind, parents who love you), how would it change the way you look at your life?

- How can your feeling grateful help others in your life?

- What does it feel like to do something nice for someone to show you appreciate that person?

- How do you respond when someone does something nice for you?

- What are some of the ways you let people know you appreciate them?

- Do you know someone who could use some praise?

- When you see someone in a bad mood, what can you do?

- When you get frustrated with yourself, what do you do?

"It is gratitude that enables us to receive and it is gratitude that motivates us to return the goodness that we have been given. In short, it is gratitude that enables us to be fully human."

—Robert A. Emmons, psychologist

8

The Touchstone of Inspiration

Helping Children Live Life with Passion!

*"Your work is to discover your world and
then with all your heart give yourself to it."*

—Buddha

Tina had always described her daughter, Lana, as a happy, bright, and "go-get-em" sort of girl. But two months into her freshman year of high school, her daughter seemed suddenly overwhelmed and seemingly unwilling to muster the motivation to keep abreast of her daily activities. Apparently Lana had a hard time adjusting to her new environment. Students from numerous other middle schools had enrolled in the high school, and Lana's close-knit group of friends from her old school seemed to drift apart as they met new people. Teachers also expect a lot more from students in high school, so Lana had to spend many more hours on homework than before. She had enjoyed playing on the soccer team in middle school, but she failed to make the team as a freshman because of the excessive competition and more experienced players. But of all these obstacles, Lana's mother worried most that her daughter seemed listless, as if she just didn't care about what she did or how she did it. She tried to motivate Lana by promising her a new outfit for every grade she pulled up by one point. She also encouraged her to bring home some new friends. When these tactics didn't work, Tina resorted to threatening Lana with groundings and the removal of privileges, but to no avail. Lana seemed to have lost her inspiration and felt dispassionate about life.

We're all familiar with those times when our children seem detached and unhappy. In Lana's case, despite the fact that she had a family who loved and encouraged her, she lost enthusiasm for life in general. Her mother's encouragement, even her attempts at reward and punishment, failed to ignite Lana's interest in the many opportunities around her. Sometimes it's difficult to figure out what motivates our children from the inside out. And, we can't live life for them—although we wish we could. Parents can't simply instill the desire to live life with zest, zeal, and ambition. Children need to feel inspired from within. So, what role can we play in that?

Lana entered the tenth grade with the same feelings of hopelessness that had haunted her through her freshman year, but thanks to a great teacher, and under the watchful eyes of a loving mother, things changed.

For Lana, a spark of interest began with the contagious enthusiasm she found in her American History teacher. He impressed her. He loved teaching, and she sensed that he deeply cared about each of his students. She felt intrigued by how facts just poured from Mr. Swede and how amazing it was that he found history interesting. Something about her teacher's passion for the subject made history come alive for Lana.

His enthusiasm captivated her. She found appealing his willingness to help his students learn to love history. He encouraged her and hinted at answers when she "sort of" knew the answer but hadn't studied the day's lesson enough. This prompted Lana to want to have "all the answers." Going the extra mile in her studies paid off, and when Mr. Swede suggested that she join the after-school history club, Lana did. The group took trips to local history sites and museums, and had lively debates about events of historic significance. Lana loved it, so much so that she campaigned to become president of the history club—and was elected!

It didn't take long for Lana's mother to notice that something about the history class not only piqued her daughter's interest, but also brought a liveliness to her that she hadn't seen for some time. Noticing that Lana's conversations became animated and excited as she discussed learning in Mr. Swede's class, Tina began to wonder what Mr. Swede knew about inspiring kids. Did he hold the key to helping Lana tap into her own special gifts and discover what truly interested her? Could her excitement about things going on in her history class spill over into other areas of life, as well? Tina arranged for a confidential meeting with Mr. Swede and shared with him how much Lana was fired up by his class. Together, they came up with some strategies for further igniting Lana's passion, in the hope that this newfound inspiration would bring back her enthusiasm for life.

Soon, Lana's joy spilled over into other areas. Her grades went up in all her classes, as did her confidence, and her outlook grew more rosy.

Lana began to believe in herself. She realized how much she enjoyed finding out all she could about how people used to live and how they struggled to grow and change through the years. She also liked sharing this knowledge with others and began to seriously consider the possibility of one day becoming a teacher herself. And, most importantly, she liked herself. She could see and feel her own joy. Her newfound passion evoked enthusiasm and zest for life, which also attracted others to her. She made new friends.

At the end of Lana's magical sophomore year in high school, she asked Mr. Swede to sign her yearbook. In it, he wrote: "You have great promise. I hope you'll work hard, go to a fine university, and help change the world."

The very next summer, Lana hung up a poster advertising her skills to teach students history during the summer break. For ten weeks that summer, and for the next two summers, she encouraged and inspired kids to not just learn a subject, but to believe in themselves and find their passion in life. Lana was loved by her young students, who came to her tutoring sessions willingly and never missed a day. Lana knew the "feel" of inspiration and its value. And it set her world ablaze with direction and purpose.

Today, Lana is a teacher of American history and her state board recently named her Teacher of the Year. In her acceptance speech, Lana paid tribute to Mr. Swede and to her mother, both of whom inspired her to live with passion. Now, she finds her ongoing inspiration from the photos of smiling students that cover the school wall. Lana has found her calling. And Mr. Swede and an attentive parent helped shine a light on the path so that she could find it.

> "Thunder is good, thunder is impressive, but it is the lightning that does the work."
>
> —Mark Twain

The Touchstone of Inspiration

A teen volunteer enthusiastically bonds with a young child from Mexico.

Wouldn't we all love to have our children always feeling enthusiastic about their lives? How great if they could live each day with vision, purpose, and passion. Certainly, we want our children to possess that magic that happens when inspiration is at work. So what defines inspiration, and how do we "teach" it? According to *Webster's Dictionary:* inspiration is a "divine influence . . . the action or power of moving the intellect or emotions." We parents want to help our children "move their intellect and emotions," but how do we do that? And do we need to wait for the divine wand of inspiration to touch our children, or can we spur this marvelous and magical zone in them ourselves? How do we help our children find and tap into their own wellspring of inspiration, so they can take delight in the beauty of a sunset, the roar of the ocean, or even feel some appreciation for the tasks and demands of life?

Children learn by example. The behaviors and attitudes parents and other adults display often influence what children learn. Tina tried to motivate her daughter's enthusiasm for life by rewarding her. But inspiration comes from within, not from without. Our goal: to raise our children with an eye toward finding and discovering what brings them the internal wealth of joy, happiness, and contentment and, from there, encourage them to seek out that which inspires them. This helps them live with zest, zeal, and excitement about life in general and all that awaits them. It is especially important for parents to be mindful about the messages we deliver about what is truly meaningful.

David Walsh, a psychologist and author of *NO: Why Kids of All Ages Need to Hear It and Ways Parents Can Say It,* contends that today's kids have "absorbed the cultural values of more, easy, fast, and fun," but that doesn't lead to happier or more content kids.[1] We want our children to appreciate the things they have, and we also want them to understand that owning certain things may bring them pleasure but has very little to do with their internal wealth. In fact, mounting evidence shows that when people chase after more and more things, they are actually less happy. External rewards can increase extrinsic motivation at the expense of intrinsic motivation. This doesn't mean that offering rewards to our children is always a negative. Sometimes rewards can help entice them to explore an activity that ends up inspiring them. But, to help our children cultivate internal joy, parents need to recognize the downside of material rewards.

According to educator Alfie Kohn, "[A] group of studies shows that when people are offered a reward for doing a task that involves some degree of problem-solving or creativity—or for doing it well—they will tend to do lower quality work than those offered no reward."[2] Receiving a reward may inspire our children to take action in the short term, but this is not true inspiration because they are taking action only to gain material things, not for internal satisfaction or because they've developed a mindset of compassion and caring. Real inspiration comes from finding the source of what interests us, from discovering our talents and our aptitudes. Finding these puts us in touch with our hearts and results in our wanting to do something because we feel compelled from within to do so—we feel inspired to act for the gratification of releasing this inner energy, and not for the gratification of receiving a reward.

We hope to bring our children an understanding of the romance of life—to feel inspired just because we have the opportunity to travel this journey of life in the first place. So how do we help our children find and live their own excitement, that joy we see when a child naturally and spontaneously opens his little mouth to catch a raindrop? Certainly, it helps if we model for our children—show them how we live our lives around those things that inspire us, and bring meaning and joy to our lives. And we can consciously make time for spontaneous moments that will bring out their sense of wonder. Julie, a parent, shares this story:

> We were driving over the mountains and into the desert. The winds blew so hard, the car was being pushed across the road. At the very top of the pass, my husband pulled off into a turnout. I looked at him, curiously.
>
> "Jump out kids," he said.
>
> For the next ten minutes our two ten-year-old boys and thirteen-year-old girl "played" in the wind. It was so strong, they could lean into it at almost a 45-degree angle and not fall to the ground. We all laughed and had a great time . . . a great break from a long drive. The kids still talk about "lying in the wind" years later. I would never have thought to stop and take in something so simple, but my husband insightfully turned a negative experience into a positive.

Our work at Kids Korps helps provide experiences for young people to get involved with others through aiding, supporting, and assisting. One of our highly prized goals comes through helping young people genuinely care about others and the world around them. And, in the process, they often find their interests, talents, and aptitudes—and act on them. This insight leads to tapping into that internal well of inspiration that resides in all of us—if only we have the opportunity to do those things that lead to its discovery. Each and every day, we see young people becoming caring, capable, competent, and joyous.

Parents often write to us about this involvement in Kids Korps, and time and again, they reiterate: When a young person gives of herself to another for no other reason than to be kind, she seems to discover something powerful within herself. Parents say when their children act from the inspiration to be kind to others, they talk about what they received, how good it made them feel, the confidence they gained, and sometimes the directional course it set for their lives. When kids take action to help others, they seem to get back more than they give.

Why Inspiration Is a Good Thing for Your Child: Six Key Benefits

Wouldn't we all like to raise kids who feel inspired to act on what brings them zest, zeal, and joy? Kids who uncover their interests and work toward perfecting their aptitudes? Kids who feel so passionate about helping others, they naturally delve into trying to learn and discover more about it? We all have within us those things we are meant to do, things that ignite our desires, fire us up, and spur us on. Yes, inspiration is a wonderful thing—and an important quality to instill in our children. When children are inspired, they:

1. "Turn on." Children who get excited about their activities will usually pursue them without prodding or needing parents to stand guard. Self-motivation can lead children to discover their innate abilities, which can help them realize their potential.

2. Increase self-confidence. When children experience the rewards of accomplishing tasks or goals that personally drive them, they feel good about themselves. This contributes to a "can-do" sense of self, sending the personal message, "I can do it. I am a capable, competent person." This positive inner message heightens their sense of confidence and personal pride in themselves. Children may not always believe in their potential when we *tell* them they can do it, but when they feel it for themselves, they will know it. This doubles back to feed their spirit of excitement, of being inspired.

3. Grow into leaders for life. Children who work toward something that inspires them actively pursue it, whether a hobby, a talent, or an aptitude. Focused energy results in accomplishment, and results in achievement. This starts a positive cycle that increases a child's sense of being a capable, competent person. Children who feel confident in their abilities become leaders in their fields and inspire others to pursue their passions.

4. Further engage their natural curiosity and sense of adventure. Inspiration helps kindle our children's curiosity and spirit of adventure. Feeling more comfortable with who they are and trusting in their inner selves can give way to a greater exploration of their passions. Delving into curiosity and adventure opens opportunities to learn and grow.

5. Increase their engagement and direction in life. Inspired children engage in many activities, and rarely feel bored. They not only look forward to doing what excites them, but they also share their excitement with others. This helps them develop the skills of communication and acceptance, as they find interest in what others want to do or accomplish.

6. Draw others to them. Children engaged in activities, setting goals, and working toward accomplishing them radiate excitement.

Others are naturally drawn to those who practice inspired actions. In turn, those children will cultivate like-minded friends in pursuit of worthy goals and who also approach living with joy and purpose—thus, creating a domino effect.

> "If you follow your bliss, you put yourself on a kind of track that has been there all the while, waiting for you, and the life that you ought to be living is the one you are living. Wherever you are—if you are following your bliss, you are enjoying that refreshment, that life within you, all the time."
>
> —Joseph Campbell, *The Power of Myth*

Helping Children "Get" the Lesson: The "Aha Shift"

When children have a positive direction for pouring their passions, they feel they can make a difference. Acting on what drives them—an internal energy from deep within their heart and soul—brings them great joy. This results in high-level achievement and a sense of great satisfaction.

Five Ways to Instill a Spirit of Inspiration in Your Child

Parents have the ability to probe our children's minds and help them get in tune with what ignites their passions. Here's how:

1. Be a model by sharing what inspires us. Show and share with your children what inspires you: cultivating friendships, running in marathons, cooking for friends and family, cycling for a cause, writing poetry, travel—whatever. Through your own excitement and positive actions, you can show your children how passions make a difference in life. Every once in a while, we may feel as if we've fallen into a rut, not spending quality time on the things that inspire us. However, when we keep focused on planting seeds of inspiration in our kids, we reignite our own spirits as well. We can't help but hear a wake-up call for ourselves. Discovering our passions together becomes both helpful and fun, which is one of the reasons for Kids Korps' success. As parents and their children go out into the community together, they discover their passions, serve others, and grow in love.

2. Take every opportunity to teach hope. Instilling hope is often undervalued. Teaching our children to move forward with positive attitudes helps them to embrace hope and to discover and feel inspired by their wishes for the future. Growing up is fraught with challenges, struggles, and uncertainties, which can make kids feel burdened. Having hope and a sense of inspiration can help lighten the load. We can teach our children that light will dispel dark moments. In addition, when they need a dose of encouragement, they can recall past moments of inspiration. As our children's strongest influence, we can bring them back to hope, over and over again.

3. Teach kids to see through an inspired lens. Inspiration gives us the ability to see something where there is seemingly nothing, the ability to create from our inner power. Often, people have the vision to create—but few take action. Wise parenting involves paying attention and looking for the little spark that fires our children's imaginations and spirits. Open a dialogue with your children's teachers, coaches, tutors, or other adults who know and have an influence in your kids' lives. Insights from others about what impassions your children can illuminate our understanding of what inspires our children. And, when they have that inspirational moment, celebrate it and encourage your kids to follow through on it. We can help children tune into abundance or a lack thereof. Good things can happen when we raise our children with the message, "Isn't life great?"

4. **Challenge your children's curiosity.** Ask children questions that encourage them to look for inspiration deep inside their hearts. The Internet or books provide good tools to help parents and children answer questions together—questions such as:

- Why is it important to help people we don't know in other countries?

- How many times did President Lincoln make mistakes before becoming one of the greatest presidents of our country?

Turn ordinary circumstances into adventures for your child—opportunities to explore the world outside, and the world within.

5. **Help children practice giving.** We might believe that inspiration is something that's either there or it's not, but we can help our children practice what makes them happy. Almost always, kids who help others feel inspired by the experience. The spark of "doing unto others" becomes the flame of compassion. The parents of Kids Korps volunteers have discovered many ways to get their children out into the community. Think about what inspires your child, and take him into the community to give to others in ways he particularly can appreciate. For example, if your child loves nature, volunteer with him through a plant-a-tree program, community garden, or park or beach cleanup project.

Is Your Child Filled with Inspiration?

Sometimes it feels like we have to coax our kids to get excited about something or feel inspired into action, or we can't seem to find anything that truly sparks their interest.

1. When your child has "nothing to do," does he:
   a. Plop down in front of the television or a video game?
   b. Follow you around, wanting you to take him somewhere or entertain him?
   c. Go to his room and set up a space station, write or read a story just for fun, or head outside to hit tennis balls on the side of the house?

2. When your child comes home from school with a research project, does she:
   a. Put off gathering information about the subject matter, miss the due date, and then complain about her failing grade?
   b. Wait until the last minute, and then come to you in a panic, expecting you to help do her work the night before the project is due?
   c. Come home excited to get on the computer or look into books, first to learn about her subject, and then create a great presentation of her work?

3. When your eight- or nine-year-old has a friend over, does she:
   a. Whine to you that they have nothing to do?
   b. Come to you after an hour of play expecting you to provide guidance?
   c. Come to you after an hour to ask when you can be an audience to watch the play they're creating?

4. When you take your child to serve food to people in need of a meal, does he:
   a. Insist on staying in the kitchen so he doesn't have to see "those people"?
   b. Station himself in the dining room and politely do his job?
   c. End up spending time with a little homeless boy he served food to, giving him the shark-tooth necklace he got on vacation last month?

Making Inspiration a Part of Everyday Life

Don't all parents want to see the spark of inspiration in their children? Magic moments of opportunity are all around us. It is a parent's privilege and responsibility to guide children toward those experiences, to help them grow and change for the good. It doesn't take much time to show our kids the magic of inspiration—only consistency.

If you have 3 minutes . . . Tell—and show—your children the meaning of inspiration by . . .

- talking openly about your own inspired moments whenever they happen;

- putting an inspirational quote in your child's lunchbox, or email (it's fast and easy—the Internet has hundreds of inspirational quotes from which to choose);

- laughing and finding humor in everyday experiences. Ask about the most inspirational thing that happened in their day;

- using the word "inspire" often when talking to your kids so they understand the concept, e.g., "That music really inspires me to take music lessons again";

- praising your child whenever it's appropriate. Your support will motivate your child to continue his successful path and maybe even help him find his passion.

If you have 30 minutes . . . Assist your child in . . .

- researching inspirational stories, with the help of the Internet and books, and have a discussion about Mother Teresa, Gandhi, Martin Luther King Jr., or talk about everyday heroes: your amazing Aunt Edna, and other "great folks" and the differences they made;

- sharing a special talent, such as singing or playing an instrument, at an orphanage or homeless shelter and remember to verbally acknowledge her talent and heart;

- starting a conversation by asking where she feels her creativity is. Then, whatever it is, encourage her to put it into action;

- exploring the unknown; e.g., together cut open a piece of fruit, remove the pit, and discuss where it might have come from, in the beginning;

- sharing inspirational quotes, stories, and poems you've collected together.

If you have 3 hours . . . As a family . . .

- do something positive with your child's skills, such as teaching a senior friend how to use a computer and the Internet;

- go to an inspirational play. Enjoy professional theater or a local children's theater;

- take in a botanical or sculpted gardens, glass blowing exhibition, etc.;

- plan a woodworking project and talk about how carving a piece of wood brings something from nothing;

- go to an arts and crafts show with your child and ask the local artists what inspires them to create their pieces of art;

- set a special time aside at home for your kids to "show-case" their artwork or favorite essay written that week. Encourage them to "brag" about their good works. Praise them and research ways to further their skills;

- learn about gardening. Pick out flowers together at the local flower mart and teach your children how to nurture the family garden;

- take your children to lunch and make "inspiration" your topic. Talk about your own accomplishments and ways you were inspired as a child, then ask them how they have been inspired and by whom;

- take your children to a poetry reading at your local book-store and discuss the message in each poem;

- take your kids to a museum and talk to them about the artwork. More important, listen to what they say about it.

If you have 3 days . . . Encourage your child to . . .

- find something that lights his fire, such as: music, acting, or sports;

- make puppets and write her own "play";

- have a karaoke or a "battle of the bands" party and select judges for the winners;

- help in the planning of a weekend outing—camping, amusement park, or touring some place. Let your child take a role in the decision-making process.

Sorting donated canned goods at the food bank can be fun!

Kids work together planting trees to beautify an urban neighborhood.

Conversation Starters for Parents and Children

- What does it mean to you to live an inspired life? What are the downsides to living an uninspired life?

- What do you do that makes you really happy inside?

- Does inspiration without action still count?

- What can you do that's creative?

- What kind of books do you like to read, and why? What is your favorite kind of music, and why?

- Do you know someone from history or current times who has lived an inspired life? What is it about that person and his/her life that is inspiring to you?

- If you were to receive bad news, what would you do about it? Can there be a silver lining in something that seems to be bad?

- What can you do to cheer someone up who is sad?

"The influence of a beautiful, helpful, hopeful character is contagious, and may revolutionize a whole town."

—Eleanor H. Porter, *Pollyanna*

PART 3

Making a Difference

Assembling beehives for indigent women in Mexico to support a micro-enterprise business

A Kids Korps family assembles a bike for a needy child.

Teens building environmentally friendly stoves in Guatemala

Having fun painting over graffiti under a local freeway

9
Inspiring Testimonials from Kids Korps USA Experiences

"I am only one; but still I am one.
I cannot do everything, but I still can do something.
I will not refuse to do the something I can do."

—Helen Keller

Over the years, we've collected numerous stories from families who greatly inspire and truly demonstrate the life-changing effects of raising kids who care about others. As these stories highlight, children who are involved in community service and volunteerism learn to help others and, in the process, become more competent, develop strong characters, and acquire a huge capacity for compassion.

Home Depot . . . and the Casa de Amparo Project

Kids Korps volunteers created projects for Casa de Amparo, a residential treatment facility for homeless and abused children.

The many types of ventures included holiday parties, outings to the zoo, and sporting events.

In 2002, Kids Korps took its relationship with Casa de Amparo a step further. Encouraged to participate in giving back, the children from Casa proved they, too, could be great volunteers.

The local Home Depot employees taught each of twelve children from Casa de Amparo how to build a simple, yet functional flower box—step by step. Upon completion, the volunteers would give the boxes to a senior in a convalescent center.

One excited teen asked, "After we make this, do we get to take it to the nursing home and meet the people who will get it?"

The mood was set, and the kids began to hammer away. In no time, everyone diligently created their own masterpiece.

Ron, the Home Depot Team Leader, encouraged the group, lending a hand with a crooked nail or a mismatched corner. Cracking a joke every ten minutes, Ron engaged the kids in lively conversation. With the energy of a lifelong teacher, Ron won their confidence and friendship. Guiding small hands, he repeatedly pulled out crooked nails and explained the use for the claw of the hammer. Patiently, Ron explained again and again how the wooden pieces fit together. Abundant smiles gleamed in response as he praised each child for a job well done.

After every participant felt satisfied they'd made a well-constructed box, the group lined up for photographs. Each child proudly held up his or her own treasure and smiled for the "Kodak moment."

Beaming from ear to ear, twelve-year-old Kristin expressed: "This is the coolest thing I've ever made."

The children left that night with their boxes and fond memories of a meaningful service-learning project. They would deliver their masterpieces to seniors in the nursing home the following Saturday.

Later, Kristin wrote about her experience:

When I Grow Up

I live in a residential facility for abused children and have been living here for four months. Since I have been here, I've learned about volunteering. It's really fun and rewarding. I especially liked making wooden boxes, painting them, and filling them with candy and flowers for an Easter basket. Delivering them was more emotional than I thought it would be. It took a lot of strength to hold back my tears, seeing these wonderful people who had been rejected, forgotten, and "put away." I know what that feels like, and it hurts a lot. I thought to myself, "Why would you disrespect or not find the time to take care of the elderly? They are wise, and they certainly know more than us!" My heart ached for the lonely men and women because I feel if you love someone, you should take care of them. That's what I'm going to do when I grow up.

They Really, Truly Believed I Was Santa Claus

I don't think I ever really comprehended how much Santa Claus meant to me as a kid until I walked into the St. Leo's Head Start Preschool Christmas party, dressed from head to toe in my red-and-white Santa attire. I was instantly surrounded by fifty little children, all wide-eyed and smiling from ear to ear, as they wrapped their arms around my legs. They were so enthusiastic that it was a miracle they didn't pull off my beard! They proceeded to lead me to the "big man's" chair where I handed them their presents. I'll never forget the look in their eyes.

Decorating holiday cookies with Head Start preschoolers

Some kids were overwhelmed with happiness; others were a bit bashful. A few began to cry because they couldn't reach me, and to be the only person around who could make their tears cease was an amazing feeling.

My close friends (dressed as elves) led each youngster, one by one, to my lap where I was able to speak to them individually. A little boy in torn jeans and an old faded green shirt jumped on my lap and said, "Can I have a stuffed animal for Christmas? My mommy and daddy said we can't afford a real pet." I reached over and grabbed the cutest little fluffy dog with a big red bow out of Santa's bag and gave it to him. His eyes widened like saucers . . . and so did my heart. One big tear glided down his small face, and I gently wiped it away with my Santa Claus mitten.

I can't put into words the warm, loving feeling I received from these children. They really, truly believed I was Santa Claus . . . the man who travels the whole world once a year and delivers presents to all . . . the man who makes one day a year a very, very special time. As I walked through the play structures waving a big good-bye and shouting "Merry Christmas" and "Feliz Navidad," I felt proud I had the opportunity to brighten each child's day with a single gift—the gift of giving of my time and heart to others. I left the experience not only feeling good about myself, but loving people more. It's true what they say about how we each have something to offer one another.

—Chris, age sixteen

Imagine a Room Like This

Imagine living in a room somewhat smaller than your bedroom, but a little bit bigger than your bathroom—and it's just a patch of dirt! In tattered old clothes with no shoes, you have to walk five miles in the 110-degree weather to get some water from the community "drinking hole," which consists of two big trash cans outside filled with hose water. The water is brownish-green with dirt at the bottom and dead bugs floating on the top. This is how the people's water really is in Mexico. Babies, as well as older children, get sick because they take baths in it. Some families drink water right out of the bucket; other families boil the water to kill germs before they drink it.

Teens happily installing a window in a newly built home in Mexico

Imagine walking around to look for items you can use to build your house: cardboard, paper, trash cans, tape, tin, and anything else you can find. After you collect scraps for your "house," you take a long walk home. You take everything you found on your walk and stack it up to build yourself a house. No joke, this is how these people really live. It is unimaginable! Most of the homes we saw can hardly be defined as a house—just simple beds and broken chairs resting on dirt floors. Many sleep under roofs made of rotting tin, and when rain and wind come, the houses can barely withstand the assault.

It's so hard to believe! People should not have to live in these conditions, and that is why our Teen Korps group went on a mission to remodel one house and fully construct another. Everyone was working so incredibly hard, and yet it really didn't feel like work. It felt like a blessing. When we saw the looks of gratitude on the faces of the family members, especially the kids, we felt so grateful for this opportunity to serve. I only wish every American teenager could have the same chance to build a home for others. This was the best experience of my life!

—Christina, age fourteen

Carving My Name

Sweating under the blazing sun, I was on my hands and knees, helping to build a house for a family in need. Two years ago, I traveled down to Aqua Prieta, Mexico, with twenty other teens on a three-day mission to build the foundation for a house. This was an experience that truly changed my life and the way I view things today. In this town, only half of the residents are employed, and the average wage is $26 per week. I had never imagined that people lived in such harsh conditions. Malnourished children ran around polluted streets with no shoes on. Most houses could hardly be defined as homes. They consisted of some uncovered mattresses and broken chairs on a dirt floor. Walls were made of cardboard and trash-can covers, while the roofs were pieces of tin, hardly enough to keep out rain or wind. Electricity was unheard of, and bathrooms were usually holes outside, right next to the water supply. In fact, Aqua Prieta means "dirty water." The brownish-green water sits in barrels outside their houses, collecting flies and mosquitoes for weeks, until eventually it is used to drink or bathe in. For a suburban American teenager, the conditions were utterly unimaginable. It was clear this community was in need of anything they could get. This trip was truly a wake-up call for me—a dose of reality.

Teens pouring a foundation for a modest home in Mexico

In the limited time we had, we accomplished a lot. We repaired houses, gave out food, distributed clothing, and built the foundation of the house. With no cement mixers, we had to hand-mix the concrete, one wheelbarrow load at a time. In order to get water, we had to walk about a mile and fill up small buckets with dirty water sitting in a large trash can. This water was mixed in the wheelbarrow with some large scoops of cement. Using a shovel, we mixed the water and the heavy cement until it formed a thick goop. Then the loaded wheelbarrow was pushed to the outline of a rectangle that we had dug earlier. The concrete was poured in and began to set. We stuck our hands into the almost-dry concrete and carved out our initials so we would forever be a part of the foundation that would hold up the house.

At first glance, it is hard to understand how people can live like that, let alone be happy with it. The kids in the community showed us that they were so happy with the littlest things in life. I have learned to appreciate everything, even things that seem so ordinary, such as shoes. I saw firsthand the things we take for granted every day. I really felt like I was making a difference. I helped build a house with my own hands. This house had a significant impact on their lives and mine. Not only did we help to put a roof over their heads, but also they helped to open our hearts. I hope to go back every year and build as many houses as possible to help out as many needy families as I can. Every time I go back, I will always know that my name was carved into the bottom of the first house I ever built.

—Dawn, age thirteen

Filling Stomachs and Touching Hearts

On Monday, June 18, I drove to downtown San Diego to feed the homeless. I had done similar projects before at St. Vincent de Paul and the Presbyterian Church, so I was not expecting to have a new or shocking experience.

Upon arrival at the Third Avenue Charitable Organization in the Lutheran Church, I noticed three or four homeless people resting outside the building. A man in a red shirt opened the door from the inside, looking at me. At once I felt out of place and like he knew why I was there. I was wearing very average clothes—a black T-shirt, jeans, and flip-flops—but what made me stand apart from him was not my clothes. I looked like I had recently had a good night's rest, a shower, and a warm meal. Clearly, these strangers could only fantasize about such things.

Young volunteers working hard to serve meals to needy families

The man in charge asked me if I needed help, and I told him I was a volunteer. He asked me to come inside. I introduced myself to the volunteers who were already chopping up potatoes, carrots, and other foods. I was led to the back of the kitchen where I washed my hands and put on an apron. One of the volunteers gave me a tour of the facility. He showed me the kitchen, the lobby where we would serve the food, and the only free medical and dental clinic in Southern California.

Then all of the volunteers gathered in the church, where one volunteer read an inspirational passage, and then the regular volunteers introduced themselves and described what we would be doing and why. Pastor Joe Lovell told us the story of how the church used to bake bread because it didn't have many members, and the plan was to use the fresh scent of bread to attract more members to their church. Instead of attracting the businessmen and families, though, it brought in herds of hungry people. Although the mal-

Taking personal pride in preparing soup at a homeless shelter

nourished were unexpected, they were still accepted into the church and given food. Feeding the homeless has been a tradition now at the Lutheran church for twenty-nine years and continues to be a great help to those in need.

As much as I enjoyed seeing these hungry people enjoying their meal, talking to the individuals themselves was even more rewarding than serving the food. We had more volunteers than we needed for serving, which gave me time to sit down outside with the homeless and chat. It was so interesting to listen to the stories of how they ended up where they were. I was deeply moved by our shared humanity and the connectedness I felt being there with them. This experience not only filled stomachs, but also touched hearts—mine, for sure.

—Patrick, age sixteen

Bowling with Love

When we signed up with our friends for the Bowl-a-Thon, we expected the day to be just like any other day of bowling, except that today we would be bowling with a bunch of kids from local shelters and foster-care facilities. Little did we know that, for these kids, it was not just an ordinary day. To go bowling was really something extra special for them. For, as a child growing up in a shelter or foster care, bowling is not often part of the plan. Most of the children were bowling for the first time ever, and with us!

The children arrived around noon. Although it was a bit hectic in the beginning, soon everyone was having a blast. One little boy in our group was obviously a bit anxious, but we helped him put his fingers in the holes of the bowling ball and showed him how to roll the ball down the alley. As he got ready to try himself, he swung the ball. "One, two, three," we counted together, and his ball went bounding down the alley. As pins fell to the lane, his face glowed. This was a proud moment indeed! We were so glad that we could witness this joy.

Teen Korps hosts a bowling party for inner-city youths.

This project really helped us to see how little things like bowling can have such a huge impact on a child's life, especially one who has struggled through a difficult past. They seemed to feel better about themselves. Without a doubt, the experience showed to us how much our small actions can influence the attitude and feelings of others.

It was strange to us that something so simple and ordinary, like bowling, was such a big deal to these children. It made us realize how much most of us take for granted. That day, we may not have won our bowling match, but what we learned was so much more rewarding and a memory we will never forget. We were so pleased to be included in such a special day of bowling with our new friends.

—Angela and Arianna, age fourteen

A Boy Named Arturo

It was summertime, warm and sunny, when I first met Arturo. My parents had informed me that I would be participating in a charity event with disadvantaged children. I had volunteered at functions before, mostly because I was told to, but on this day in particular, I complained bitterly about giving up my Saturday. "I already have plans!" I remember protesting to my mother.

I shudder when I recall my selfish attitude that day. I agreed to go, but did so grudgingly, and I punished my parents with my negative demeanor and surly behavior.

After arriving at the event, I was immediately partnered with a young boy named Arturo. His head hung low as he was introduced to me, and it was clear that he had resisted this meeting as much as I had. He kept his arms crossed against his chest tightly as his foster parent nudged him in my direction. Arturo avoided my eyes at first, and we scowled at each other when we finally made eye contact. My own irritation lessened as I recognized a look that told me this boy had been thrust upon strangers more times than he could count. As I knelt down to ask him to help plan our day, a slow smile crept to his lips. His ability to stay angry evaporated, as did mine, when we both realized that since we were stuck with each other, we might as well make the best of it. As we walked together, exploring the area, his little hand reached up to grab mine, and my heart began to swell. This child was depending on me to provide him with a respite from his troubled life. By giving of myself, I was actually changing his outlook on life, at least for the day. My regrets about not being home, talking on the phone, or using the computer were at once dismissed, and I realized the real importance of what was happening.

Arturo and I skipped along, had lunch together, and even went to a place where we created our own stuffed animal.

Arturo chatted with me about things that are important only to a young boy, and I listened like I had never listened to anyone before.

The day seemed to speed by and, before we knew it, we realized it was time for the day to end. Arturo clung to me silently, reluctant to let this special time end. Tears welled up in our eyes as we said goodbye, and I promised Arturo he would have more special days in his future.

As I looked into the eyes of this child, I had realized that although Arturo may have benefited from spending the day with me, I had gained far more. The thought that I had almost missed this chance to spend the day with Arturo made me sad. My parents had always told me that giving was more gratifying than receiving but, on this day, I finally understood what this meant. I was so thankful to them for insisting that I participate. This little boy, Arturo, had taught me a lot and allowed me to grow into a person who is willing to reach out to others in need and discover a part of myself that has always been there.

Having the opportunity to give of myself in order to enrich the lives of others is now something I seek out, and I have Kids Korps and a boy named Arturo to thank for teaching me this.

—Kyle, age fifteen

Bare Whitewashed Walls

One morning, when I woke up, I dared not open my eyes. I was frozen stiff, terrified, hoping the night before was nothing more than a bad dream. When I finally mustered the courage to pry open my eyelids, the first thing I encountered were bare whitewashed walls. As I slowly became conscious of my hospital surroundings, I noticed my mother by my side, quietly weeping. Suddenly, I felt overwhelmed by a strange fear—fear of the unknown. She gently told me that I had been diagnosed with the autoimmune disease called juvenile diabetes. Diabetes? I was only ten years old. What was diabetes, and why did I have it? My mind started racing, disturbed by the thought that my life would never be the same.

However, while I was in Children's Hospital for my initial treatment of diabetes, I had a revelation that would forever change my role in the community.

One day I ventured to the hospital's playroom, expecting nothing more than some interaction with other kids. When I arrived, I was shocked and felt strangely uncomfortable with the image of children playing in such a gloomy place.

I spent the day with many terminally ill children, but the majority of my time went to one special girl. I vividly remember playing the board game Chutes and Ladders with this young girl who was battling leukemia. She had no hair as a result of her treatments, and she was connected to a portable intravenous system. At the conclusion of our game, I rushed back to my hospital room where I cried for hours, thinking of this amazing young girl who had incurable cancer that would soon claim her life. There was absolutely nothing she could do about it.

Volunteeres entertain kids who are less fortunate.

Feeling helpless, I asked myself, "Why?"

I could not think of any fair

answer, but I realized I was extremely fortunate to have a situation that was controllable, and I should never pity myself for having diabetes.

From that point on, I decided to devote a significant amount of my time to helping improve conditions for those less fortunate in my community. I became actively involved as a leader in community service, spending hundreds of hours over the past seven years attempting to make people's lives just a little better. Nothing is more rewarding than bringing a smile to the face of an abused child or a lonely senior.

If that one morning when I awoke to whitewashed walls had been a bad dream after all, I might have missed out on some of the most important and rewarding moments I have ever experienced while helping others. I attribute the wonderful experiences I've had and contributions I've made to my little friend in the hospital, to having the disease that helped me learn the meaning of compassion.

—Jarred, age seventeen

Flowers to Remember

Our town has Habitat for Humanity homes, and a few years ago, a bunch of us at the Boys and Girls Club volunteered to make flower boxes for the new residents. The Home Depot store had arranged to teach us how to construct, paint, and then plant flowers in the boxes. We had so much fun that day, putting everything together. I remember that day so well because I had never volunteered before.

The next day we delivered our gifts. When we arrived with cars full of flower boxes, we didn't know what to do at first. We each took a box and walked up to one of the new homes. Some of the residents peeked out their new front windows, not knowing what to think about a big group of kids delivering flowers. Others did not open their doors because they were new to this country and had no idea what we were up to.

I walked up the freshly laid steps of a house that had been completed just days before and knocked on the door. There were no trees or grass yet, and the driveway still had to be paved. I was a little nervous at first. Would they slam the door in my face? To my surprise, when they opened the door, they had big grins on their faces. They stepped out, and I handed them my box. Then, all of a sudden, the woman wrapped her arms around me and gave me a great big hug. She was crying and smiling all at the same time. She looked like I had just given her a million dollars. I think I was just as excited as she was.

Boys & Girls Club volunteers deliver flower boxes to residents of Habitat for Humanity homes.

We sat down on her steps and talked for a while, and I learned that they, like me, were new to the country. The woman said my gift was the best welcome to America she ever had! When we left the Habitat for Humanity neighborhood that afternoon, we smiled at our work. It was like we were looking at a painting: new houses with lots of flower boxes dotting the landscape. What a beautiful sight it was!

I'll never forget the feeling I had that day. I had a chance to give to someone else, and I felt good, really good about it. So did my friends, who asked the Kids Korps leader when we would do our next project.

—Tawnya, age thirteen

I Wished upon a Shooting Star

Dear My New Soldier Friend,

I think you are so brave and honorable, and I look up to you. I know that going to war is not easy, and I am thankful for your sacrifice. I know you will get through it and live a long and happy life. I have faith in you. Last night I saw a shooting star, and I wished for you and your soldier friends to be okay and come home safely. I hope that one day I, too, can serve my country and make myself useful. So when you get down, or are feeling lonely, just remember that you have a friend in California always thinking of you. Happy Valentine's Day!

—Elliott, age ten

Testimonials from Kids Korps Leaders

School isn't all ABCs and 123s. Teachers also help build character in our children. In February, our kids changed priorities, from eating Valentine's candy to reaching out; the entire kindergarten through sixth grade classes at our school created heartfelt valentines and letters honoring our overseas military. More than 600 letters were sent through Operation Independence to cheer on those who were overseas, away from their loved ones, serving our country.

The children wrote touching, sweet, creative, and sometimes just plain funny letters they addressed to "Dear Friend" or "Dear Soldier," and others, to "Dear American Hero," "My Inspiration," "My New Soldier Friend," "Guardian of America," "Dear Warrior," and "Dear Protector."

Most of the letters thanked the service personnel for their tremendous sacrifices and bravery, showed great empathy for the fact that the soldiers fought so far away from family and friends, and hoped the soldiers would soon arrive home safely.

Some of the children mentioned they had relatives serving in Iraq, and many had grandfathers who had served in other wars.

Some serious letters described what freedom meant to them.

A few expressed reservations about the war in Iraq, but still showed great respect and caring for the troops.

Others wrote about themselves, their hobbies, pets, favorite subjects, and goals.

At least a few dozen said, "You rock!"

Many of the cards had silly jokes, riddles, and poems.

Some of the younger boys asked how much the soldiers' guns weighed and said that war looked a lot harder than video games.

The children decorated cards with lots of hearts, flags, and other artwork. They signed their cards, "A Special Friend," "From your Fellow Citizen," or simply, "Love." The valentines and letters demonstrated as many good qualities about the children who wrote them as about the troops who would receive them. Our young volunteers have certainly earned an A in character for their compassion, enthusiasm, and encouragement.

—Diana, Kids Korps Chapter Leader

Upon leaving the El Cajon New Alternative Residential Treatment Center, I felt overcome by bittersweet emotions. I slipped into my now empty car, once filled with Christmas trees, arts-and-crafts projects, cookies, and gifts. The laughter-filled day had overflowed with excitement and joy, as our Kids Korps members enthusiastically touched the lives of each child with their gifts and, more important, their time. Arts and crafts, cookie decorating, and a visit from Santa, all made these sometimes forgotten children feel special. Weeks of planning by our Teen Korps board members and the generous gift purchasing from all the Kids Korps families helped to make it a successful event.

My thirteen-year-old daughter seemed to experience the same mixed feelings as I. With a long sigh, she said, "Thanks, Mom. That was such a great day! It was so nice seeing the happy faces on these kids. I only wish we could do more."

Silently, we all thought for a moment.

Then I heard my eight-year-old son's mousy voice say, "Yeah, thanks, Mom, and thank you for being my mom."

I could feel a great big lump in my throat and an excited feeling in my stomach as I drove. I realized this exemplified what Kids Korps is all about. These are the types of moments and experiences we hope to give to our kids—the acts of compassion and empathy for others, and the realization that the world revolves around all, not just them.

At times, with our hectic schedules, we question ourselves as Teen Korps leaders: "Why have I taken this on? Am I nuts?"

Today, I knew deep in my heart that it's all worth it. As I looked in the rearview mirror at my sleeping kids, exhausted from a day of giving to others, I felt so proud about what they had experienced and how they had impacted others' lives. And I also felt blessed by how our own lives had changed for the better.

—Leeann, Parent Team Leader

It occurred to me, somewhere between Tijuana and Ensenada, Mexico, how a small change can make a huge difference. Twenty-nine Kids Korps volunteers would spend the next forty-eight hours focused on building a home for a family of five in a colonia outside of Ensenada. In the larger scheme of life, two days is not much time, but our two days of effort could make a big difference to the Santiago family.

As we headed south across the border, I imagined the family's anticipation of our arrival. They lived in a makeshift house with dirt floors. We learned the family of five slept in a space barely large enough for the one set of bunk beds they all slept in—mom, dad, and baby on the queen-sized bottom, and the two older kids together on top. Their only other room, a kitchen/living area, was not much larger. In the blink of an eye, we would return to San

Diego, leaving them a home growing to more than double the size of their current one. Their new home would also have a cement floor, instead of dirt, which, we were told, would cut illnesses by half.

As our weekend unfolded, I watched the commitment of our group. Everyone worked with purpose. Dust clung to sweaty arms and faces, and the energy clearly flowed toward something larger. Imagine: eleven families with children from ages six to sixteen, all focusing in one direction. While intense, the working together that weekend brought with it an understanding of the power of giving, and the entire group seemed to know they were receiving at least as much as, and maybe more than, the Santiagos.

How truly heartwarming, watching our young volunteers work alongside each other: A girl of fourteen installed the electrical wiring, apprenticed by her dad; mothers worked on the roof with their sons; dads put up

Youth With A Mission (YWAM) gives kids the opportunity to help others.

drywall with their daughters; siblings worked together, with a constancy almost any parent would find boggling; almost everyone came together to raise walls and lift the roof; even our two smallest volunteers, age six, painted walls. The hard work didn't let up, nor did the positive spirit.

Shortly before we'd finished for the day, Mr. Santiago looked at me and told me how the weekend was a miracle to him. Wiping his eyes, he said, "You come here and do this, wanting nothing from us in return. I will always remember . . ."

As "our" home came close to completion, the two six-year-olds gave up painting walls and busily made treasures with scraps of wood. Makaela made a very creative nail block, and Julia painted a perfect wooden heart, which one of the fathers had skillfully sawed for her. Bigtha, the Youth With A Mission (YWAM) coordinator, observed the girls proudly showing off their work, eager to take their creations home. She took the girls aside, dropped to their level, and told them how children like the Santiago children did not have toys. They found things, like the wooden scraps, and put them together to make things to play with.

Building a house in Mexico is a rewarding team experience.

Julia and Makaela, with the help of twelve-year-old Nikki, set about immediately nailing together whatever their little minds could create and put "toys" together for the children.

The completion of the Santiago house was met with beaming satisfaction. As we readied ourselves to leave, everyone glowed.

Little six-year-old Julia wanted to say good-bye to the kind Santiago "Mama," who had not only made us lunch each day, but thanked and hugged our children with warmth and graciousness. Holding tightly to the little heart she had made, Julia went to Mrs. Santiago and said, "Adios."

Mrs. Santiago took Julia's little face in her hands and said something softly in Spanish. Then she lifted Julia's heart from her hands. "Ah . . . es muy bonita, Julia. ¿Es para mi?" she asked gently.

"Honey," I said, "the mama is saying she really likes your heart and she's wondering if you want to keep it, or if it's for her." (Julia loved the little heart she had made, so I wasn't sure if she would just want to show it to "Mama" or give it to her.)

Julia looked back and forth at us, then looked at me, and said, "I want to give this to the mama."

Everyone on this trip had similar feelings of generosity, not just our youngest builders. One family had lost a son who had been a Kids Korps volunteer before he died. They experienced this trip as a legacy to him. Other parents felt privileged to see their children work so hard to help others. The power of giving seemed to touch the entire group.

When Julia got home, she said to her dad, "You know what? We built a house for a family, a whole house, Daddy—and at the end I gave my heart to the mama, and she cried."

—Sharon, Kids Korps Team Leader

These heartfelt sentiments are important because kids and their parents took the opportunity to articulate how they felt about their experiences when giving to others. The stories give us a sneak peak into their hearts and minds, helping us understand what's most meaningful to them.

Through these stories, we continue to see how the five touchstones—Interdependence, Connection, Perspective, Gratitude, and Inspiration—contribute to children becoming compassionate, loving human beings who genuinely care about and for others.

The "Aha Shift" evident in these stories demonstrates that kids have learned fundamentally and profoundly that the best way to take care of themselves is to take good care of others.

10

Kids Korps USA

More Than a Decade of Teaching Kids to Care

"Those of us who are in this world to educate—to care for—young children have a special calling that has very little to do with the collection of expensive possessions but has a lot to do with the words inside of heads and hearts. In fact, that's our domain: the heads and hearts of the next generation, the thoughts and feelings of the future."

—Fred M. Rogers, late host
of **Mr. Roger's Neighborhood**

Kids Korps, a nonprofit youth volunteer organization, does precisely what this book describes: teaches kids to care. Each of the authors has, in some way, intimately involved herself with the formation and support of the organization, and the insights come from observing youth volunteers in action for more than twelve years. Kids Korps activities serve as examples of ways to instill in our kids the spirit of giving. But while this wonderful organization helps thousands of children and their families do wonderful deeds, it is by no means the only way to engage children in acts of giving. (Appendix A offers resources for engaging children to step beyond their personal needs.)

> The world is only as great as the people who step forward to serve others. Through thousands of community outreach projects, Kids Korps has made a lasting, positive impact in the communities served. Their army of young volunteers has delivered hot food to the homeless, provided relief to the ill and disabled, cared for seniors and tended to our environment and animals in need. We applaud all of the children whose caring and hard work has made each community service a success. They represent the next generation of our country's leaders, and their involvement in the community is a big part of reaching their highest potential.
>
> —Arnold Schwarzenegger, Letter of Recognition to Kids Korps

Build It and They Will Come: Kids Korps and Its Vision

The big hit movie, *Field of Dreams* (1989) with Kevin Costner, held a message of hope: "Build it and they will come." Its success stemmed from the positive force that guided the story. The sweet, inspirational movie is about an Iowa farmer who builds a baseball diamond in his cornfield, according to what he believes are the instructions of voices he hears. When he does, the long-deceased 1919 Chicago White Sox players (who became known as the Black Sox after they threw the World Series) make a comeback. The underlying message: "If you believe in the impossible, the incredible will happen."

It's true. We know, because it happened to us.

The idea of Kids Korps came about one day in 1994. Cofounder Joani Wafer found herself in the midst of a particularly troubling moment. She had watched her kids—then aged five, seven, and eight—play video games, for hours. When she tried to start a conversation with them, they'd reply something like: "Yeah, Mom, whatever you want." But, of course they didn't budge.

Glued to electronics, each child had entered their own world, ignoring the beautiful day outside. Their self-absorption bothered her.

"What can I do to help them get outside themselves?" she wondered.

Out of nowhere, she experienced a vision of smiling and laughing children gathered together, serving other people in need. At that moment, the words "children for charity" came to her mind. She immediately "got it." Her kids didn't care enough about the world outside of their stuff. They knew how to *take* very well, but did they know how to give?

Joani's kids had everything—a loving family and material comforts galore. In those moments, she wondered what kind of adults they would turn into. Would they focus only on themselves or would they engage in meaningful connections, doing things with and for others? Was she raising kids the world would embrace and need? Would her kids feel happy and purposeful if they didn't learn how to get outside themselves? These unsettling thoughts would give rise to Kids Korps USA, an organization designed to help parents find answers to the type of questions that plagued her that morning in the kitchen.

Within hours of envisioning a children's volunteer organization, Joani talked with some close friends about her concerns. She discovered she wasn't alone. All agreed, their children and community could indeed benefit from participating in youth-involved service activities.

In their discussions, questions arose: "What can we do to help our children understand what it's like to help others, to care whether or not some people are disadvantaged, hungry, poor, or in need of a friend?" And, "How can they learn this when they themselves live in nice houses, in safe and manicured neighborhoods, with parents protecting them from the harsh realities of life or, at the least, from seeing the other side of the coin?"

The next day, Joani flew to North Carolina to tell her sister, Dawn Lehman, about her concerns and her vision. That night at dinner, they started to think about names that captured the concept of kids coming together to help others.

They asked each other: "How can we start an organization for kids when we have no experience in the nonprofit world? And who would help us get it started?" *Field of Dreams* came to mind, and they said, "Hey, why not? Let's build it and see if they come." Kids Korps USA, a nonprofit youth volunteer organization with headquarters initially in San Diego, California, and Chapel Hill, North Carolina, was born that night.

The next week, Dawn and Joani set out to talk to more parents. Parent after parent asked them: "How can we teach our children that there is more to life than buying toys and playing video games?" "How can we show them the importance of depending on one another?" "How can we get our children to be more grateful?" "What will inspire kids to step outside themselves to help others?" "How can we keep our kids from becoming statistics, from succumbing to the boredom, drugs, and violence swooping down on so many young people today?"

By the end of the week, a kernel of an idea became an action plan taking root in their communities. On a Saturday morning, Joani and Dawn gathered a group of friends and their kids and hauled them off to do some "community good" at a senior convalescent home.

The local nursing home was the last place eight-year-old Matt wanted to be at nine o'clock on a Saturday morning. He lagged behind, with his mom's hands pushing his ironing-board-stiff back. His feet dug imaginary skids into the floor just inside the door, and his nose rumpled as he took a resistant breath. "Pee-yew! It smells like medicine, hospital food, and urine all mixed together."

Then, with his head lowered, he scoped out the room. Old people sitting in wheelchairs circled a small group of kids who'd already started fitting in. They were the home's first youth volunteers. Some oldsters slumped sideways in their chairs; others leaned slightly forward, as though about to fall out of their chairs at any moment.

When Matt noticed one man's eyes fixed on him—no smile, no nod, just a blank stare—he lowered his head further, shifting his stance every couple of seconds.

Matt's mom gently pushed him forward again, and he reluctantly made his way toward the group of kids already in the center of the wheelchair circle. He slowly raised his arms to match the others as the young volunteers scooped and bent and raised their bodies in a chain of aerobic movements. The wheelchaired residents matched the children's swift movements the best they could.

Next came the helium balloon volleyball exercise. As instructed, Matt carefully volleyed an air balloon to his senior partner. If patted correctly, the ball would help the senior exercise his fingers, hands, and arms. Matt connected with his partner in the rhythm of the volley. His face relaxed, and his mouth revealed a hint of a smile. His partner's eyes gleamed.

Standing in the corner of the room, his mother watched her son's every movement. His body moved back and forth like a pendulum; his spread fingers slightly pushed and caught the red air ball. With every move, Matt further connected with himself and his partner. Touched by this gentle side of her son—a side she'd barely glimpsed before, his mother wiped away a tear.

Matt had gained a new perspective on older adults.

When the other parents saw the tears rolling down Matt's mother's face, many also began to cry. They realized, "Oh, my God, something special has just happened here. We need to do this again—for our children, for *all* children."

So ended the very first Kids Korps volunteer activity and, of course, other experiences followed. The following week in Chapel Hill, Dawn recruited ten children from a Boys and Girls Club to visit the elderly at a local senior center.

Bingo! "Again," Dawn recalls, "magic took place in the act of giving."

First, the young volunteers hung a large handmade "Have a happy day!" poster in the activity center for all to see. Then, as they moved from room to room introducing themselves and presenting greeting cards, a youthful, uplifting energy brushed the stale air. Once more, an amazing connection—beyond words—took place.

Residents in wheelchairs reached out to touch the youth, and the youth responded by holding their hands. The many enthusiastic smiles invited the kids to visit again, which they later did—with remarkable respect and compassion.

Young volunteer Matt later said: "I learned that old people could be good friends. Some old people look sad, but you could make them happy."

Kids Korps: On a Mission

A wonderful thing happened when the Kids Korps volunteers went out into the community to serve. They started the steps in becoming leaders in their groups and in their communities.

We've discovered that participation in Kids Korps provides a key ingredient to personal growth, because our young volunteers learn the five touchstones we've talked about in this book: interdependence, connection, perspective, gratitude, and inspiration.

Thus our mission succeeds in filling their hearts with the spirit of giving. For more than a decade we have seen these five attitudes and behaviors build character and compassion, give youth a positive identity, instill a sense of purpose, and connect family and community—exactly what we and our friends wanted.

Kids Korps made it easy for children and families to participate in community service, and parents discovered that serving others, together, strengthened family bonds. Then something else started to happen. Kids began developing an inner strength. Parents began to tell us how their Suzie showed up for a friend in need, or their Dan helped out at home more, or their Elizabeth stood up in a group and said, "I don't agree with all of you making fun of Seth," even though she hardly knew him. Not only did parents have more "feel good" moments with their kids, but their children also behaved in new ways, making a difference to others. Needless to say, this pleased everyone.

Giving: A Habit of the Heart

Kids Korps set out to help parents consciously raise kids who care, but how could we get kids involved? We all know the challenges in finding an activity that won't turn them off. So we experimented and came up with many fun and exciting projects: building bikes to give to the less fortunate, going bowling with kids with disabilities, and stuffing duffle bags with necessities for foster children. Year after year, we discovered a pattern in our volunteers' behavior: The more they served others, the more the giving turned into a habit of their hearts.

Teen Korps counselor connects with Head Start preschoolers

**Parents and their children
complete the assembly
of a bike for a child in need.**

**Kids team up in an
assembly line production
to fill duffel bags
for abused children.**

The key to successful campaigns in the public relations and advertising worlds is, in three words: frequency, frequency, frequency. Too often a campaign fails because the client tires of the message and wants to change it. In reality, when the client's interest wanes, the campaign has just begun to sink into the minds of the consumer. Think about some of the musical advertising slogans that have aired for years, such as "Got milk?"; Campbell's Soup is "M'm! M'm! Good!"; and Maxwell House's "Good to the last drop." What about General Electric's "We bring good things to life" and United Airlines' "Fly the friendly skies of United"? Most of us can identify these products as soon as we hear the opening jingle of the commercial! Sometimes we even go about our daily activities humming the tune.

The same thing holds true for engaging our kids in giving. The more they do it, the more they will make it a part of their life. They get hooked on service. Here's a story from Nicole, age thirteen:

Instead of saying I volunteer to make a difference in the world, I would have to start off by saying just the opposite. Volunteering has made a difference in me. Through Kids Korps, I have been able to take on projects

160

and be exposed to places where I never would have gone or even have been able to imagine going to, throughout my entire life. You often hear people sympathizing for the unfortunate, but sending out sympathy through thoughts and words is not what gets things done. Taking action is what makes the difference, and the impact is not the same until you are actually there yourself. It makes a world of a difference when you are on the scene. You feel and understand every level and degree of things that you suddenly realize you had no idea about before.

Through volunteering, I was able to add a deeper understanding and a new perspective to my outlook and thoughts. I think volunteering is not only about people helping others. Actually, I would say the people you help and the experience of it improve and change the type of person you are just as much as, or maybe even more than, what one could ever do for someone else. Volunteering with Kids Korps has given me the chance to get to know more about myself. I have a new appreciation for my life, and the more things I do, the more I learn about the world and how just a little compassion can go a long way— not just for the world, but for my own good as well. Volunteerism does make a difference to the world, but more important, it makes a difference to me. And that is what Kids Korps has added to my life.

We used to think that children learned caring only as they grew into adulthood. Some researchers now believe that children can show signs of empathy and concern from an early age. Kids Korps encourages children to volunteer starting at age five, because we've discovered, if given the opportunity, kids as young as kindergarteners can really "see" the world outside themselves. They react responsibly, wanting to help "fix" a problem; they offer comfort and compassion to a parent with a headache, for example.

When a Kids Korps mom talked with her five-year-old Ashley about their experience at an orphanage, the child's ability to understand other kids' needs made her smile. "Mommy, next time we come back, can I bring my friend some of my old toys?"

If we can put kids in school at age five and take them to Sunday school at age three, why can't we get them out in the community to help others as soon as they seem ready, regardless of age? Isn't *learning to give* another important aspect of children's education?

Even though we initially touted "If we build it, they will come," when we started Kids Korps, we thought it would grow as a grassroots organization in two cities. We'd find a couple of moms to help out and gather a few handfuls of kids to serve at the local homeless shelters. But, they did come—hundreds and hundreds. We received telephone calls from parents and teachers and youth groups. Some of the parents responded because when their kids heard about Kids Korps at school they wanted to join. Word got out. Soon, newspaper and magazine articles and the television news carried our agenda. Wow! The unimaginable turned into the incredible! It became quite obvious: There was a need in the community, Kids Korps helped to fill it, and we've been doing it ever since.

We created Kids Korps to help kids journey a little deeper into their hearts and souls to discover their individual uniqueness and what they can do with their lives, by giving to others. The overall philosophy: When we help children develop their innate capabilities to give to others, they reveal to us their prowess to grow into stronger, more well-rounded kids. Isn't that what we all want for our kids?

Our Incredible Kids

Kids Korps makes volunteering easy. Parents have fun in their endeavors while getting their family involved in community services:

- painting over graffiti
- cleaning up parks and waterways
- serving food at soup kitchens
- making gifts for the homeless and needy

- delivering Meals-On-Wheels treats

- helping to refurbish buildings in low-income areas

- recycling materials to create new products

- making scooters for people with disabilities

- visiting people in hospitals, nursing homes, and battered women's and children's homes

Our kids quickly learn that the service they provide impacts real people, and they feel good about it. From Emily, age seventeen:

It's one thing to give material goods to help someone in time of need, but it's quite another to give part of your heart. I've helped build and furnish houses in Mexico for families who had previously been living under a makeshift shelter of plastic sheeting; I've tutored kids at orphanages; I've helped keep score at Special Olympics competitions; and I've cleaned hundreds of pounds of trash off California beaches. After hand delivering a Thanksgiving meal to a needy family and seeing their sincere appreciation for my small gesture, I was filled with pride because I gave back to my community. The family's two little girls beamed as they showed me the paper and crayon holiday ornaments they had made. I fought back tears as I saw the ornaments through their eyes: priceless labors of love, more special than anything you can buy at the finest store.

I know how truly lucky I am.

In the beginning, I felt ill-equipped for the task. What could one kid do when confronted with a bunch of needy strangers? I wasn't even very good at picking up my own dinner dishes—and now I was asked to pick up someone else's, too. I did it only because my family and friends were involved, but I got swept up into something wonderful.

Today, I reflect and understand how I've been empowered into action and how one person can make a difference. I would never have believed it possible. Efforts to change can inspire others to follow in others' footsteps, down a path that will eventually lead to a better world. I've seen it. I've contributed. I've learned a lesson: the power of one.

As Kids Korps continues to grow, our vision is the same as it was twelve years ago: to encourage children to have a broader *perspective* on life, to give them opportunities to *connect* with others, to show them the importance of *interdependence,* to let them see the results of *inspiration,* and, above all, to nurture a *grateful* heart. We've seen what happens to kids who give. We've watched their attitudes and behaviors change—for the better—and take pride in the many who have become young adult leaders. We didn't tell them they had to be the president of Teen Korps or the president of the Philanthropy Club at the University of Michigan or the president of a sorority at Stanford, but, in the process of giving to others, they became these leaders. They came to realize the power of one!

The Value of Kids Korps for Your Child

We're fond of telling the story about the woman who planted flower seeds in her garden. After a few months, she noticed that most of the bed flourished—the brightly colored flowers, big and robust. One small part of the garden, however, had not grown. Rather than find out what happened to impede the growth of the diminished part, the woman decided to find out what strengthened the flourishing side. That way she would know what to do to help the other. She discovered that when the roots grew deep enough, the seed would become a beautiful blossom. (Apparently, the seeds in the barren area had never taken root and lacked nourishment.) Just as seeds emerge out of healthy soil to rise as flowers in a garden of color, Kids Korps gives its volunteers the opportunity to grow out of a nurturing environment, with deeply rooted values, to see the world outside of self.

We have also noticed how many young volunteers, when given the opportunity, enjoy *mentoring* other kids who want to volunteer. One of the most moving moments we've shared came when a group of Boys and Girls Club members (also Kids Korps volunteers) taught kids with disabilities how to volunteer.

While at the Home Depot store, two ten-year-old boys helped a fifteen-year-old girl, who was blind, with her contribution. She used a hammer and nails, painted a box, and planted flowers—all for the first time in her life. The club members reacted with empathy, patience, and pride. No one noticed her lifeless eyes when she laughed with delight over her accomplishment.

Every week, the bus ride home for the Kids Korps volunteers was unlike anything the Boys and Girls Club director had ever seen. A serene calm filled the bus as the young volunteers talked about the people they'd mentored. Without prompting, they shared stories with each other and discussed their new friends. A wonderful interdependence had taken place: The kids with disabilities needed someone to help them volunteer, and the Kids Korps volunteers enjoyed feeling needed.

Within a short time after Kids Korps volunteers went into action, word spread around the schools. Kids went home and asked their moms if they could join Kids Korps. "It was the cool thing to do."

The Kids Korps phones started ringing off the hook. Those first volunteers became *models* for the next group of kids, and the next group of kids became models for the third wave of new volunteers, and so on.

Another exciting thing that happened over the years involved the seasoned teen volunteers. They wanted to serve the community with kids their own age, wanted to design and work their own projects, and preferred to decide for themselves how they would become *advocates* for their community; thus began Teen Korps. Remember Matt, the young boy who didn't want to go to the nursing home? He became the president of one of the Teen Korps chapters.

We realized that a whole evolution had taken place with our Kids Korps members. They had gone way beyond the first service-learning steps (learn, serve, and reflect) to integrate their experiences, mentor

A teen mentors youth in community outreach responsibility as they fill disaster preparedness kits for low-income families.

Teen mentor helping a young volunteer develop craftsmanship skills

other young volunteers, model the Kids Korps values, and advocate for their community. We now call this path the *seven critical steps for developing leaders for life:* learn, serve, reflect, integrate, mentor, model, and advocate.

In a profound way, in taking these steps, the Kids Korps volunteers learned the five touchstones we talk about in this book—*interdependence, connection, perspective, gratitude,* and *inspiration*—and became more well-rounded, caring people.

Volunteerism Is a Family Affair

Parents who introduce Kids Korps to their schools tell us Kids Korps has successfully developed a wonderful, hands-on character-education program that teaches trustworthiness, respect, fairness, honesty, responsibility, citizenship, and caring. We know this is good stuff, and kids who have volunteered will vouch for it, but we also know some kids need motivation and encouragement to volunteer. Parents who integrate the touchstones into their everyday lives raise kids who will get the most out of service-giving activities.

Our observations of Kids Korps families working together support studies showing that the volunteering habits of the family—particularly the parents—have a significant impact on the volunteering habits of youths. A November 2005 study by the Corporation for National and Community Service demonstrated that parents' volunteering activities influence the likelihood that youth will volunteer during their childhood and later in adulthood. By volunteering, parents become role models for community involvement.[1]

The concept of giving and servicing is not new. The "newness" comes in the heightened awareness of service as the *foundation for building character in our children, strengthening families,* and *creating more socially connected communities.*

"Build it and they will come."

Yes, they came—and they stayed. Over the years, many parents, teachers, school administrators, and youth organization leaders have told us they feel fortunate to have Kids Korps in their community. They love the idea of mobilizing children to serve in wonderful ways, and they can see the difference the children make in the lives of others.

Volunteerism becomes even more worthwhile when families serve together, because it brings family members closer to one another—to talk, to share, to care. Both kids and parents often tell us about the special family times—more meaningful than they ever expected. Whether we choose our local volunteer center, our schools, our places of worship, or Kids Korps as our venue for engaging in service, we are taking big steps toward raising kids to care and are preparing them to lead the way to a better, more tolerant, and more compassionate world.

11

Creating a "Caring Epidemic" in Your Community

Be the Difference; Make the Difference

What a delight, to look into the wide eyes of a child in the midst of expressing wonder, excitement, and the sheer appreciation that comes from experiencing the true joy of helping others. We've seen those eyes over and over again, and we've heard the genuine stories that kids of all ages share about their feelings of connection, accomplishment, and gratefulness when they see the world from the perspective of what they have to offer of themselves to others. Developing compassion and respect for the world empowers our children to act, individually and collectively.

Inviting a caring mindset into our homes certainly brings joy to our kids and to our families. But doing so also gives us a chance to move beyond our individual families and put "altruism" and "giving back" into our collective vocabulary. The mindset of caring transcends the family unit and has much larger social implications. So, as parents, if we want a warmer, gentler society, how can we start a positive epidemic? How do we initiate public change?

A young volunteer proudly finishes his handmade blanket for homeless children.

Though we have no magic bullet to cure the ills of society, we can take action to strengthen the communities where we live. As parents and citizens, we have the power not only to create a positive family environment for our children, but also to change our communities for the better. And, in doing so, we become shining examples for teaching our kids to give. Through giving, they turn into catalysts of change. In much the same way as citizens connect and care for one another, children grow from healthy interaction. According to sociologist Robert Putnam, the correlation between high social investments and positive child development comes as close to perfection as social scientists ever find.

If you're thinking, "What can I do? I'm just one person," think about how change so often starts through the conviction of one person. When a drunk driver killed Candace Lightner's thirteen-year-old daughter, she started Mothers Against Drunk Driving (MADD) and changed the way a nation responds to drinking and driving. Michael Josephson, who surveys thousands of teens annually about ethics and moral behavior, has made a difference by developing a character education program, now used throughout the nation. He left a thriving law practice to found Character Counts! in large part because he didn't want to raise his children in a morally equivocal world. These are only two parents who, because of their own children, found the motivation to make a stand for positive change for all children. Each of them has started a caring epidemic that has added to the well-being of society—and they represent merely two of a very long list.

Starting a Movement

By modeling parents like Candace Lightner and Michael Josephson, we can inspire empathic thinking in our children, which can lead to life-changing events. And not just parents, youths can take the lead, too. Take, for example, the story of Craig Kielburger.

One morning before school, twelve-year-old Craig picked up the *Toronto Star*. While looking for the comics section, a front-page article caught his eye. The article told of Iqbal Masih, a young boy from Pakistan, sold into child labor at the age of four to pay a family debt. Iqbal worked six days a week, twelve hours a day, received little food, and was sometimes chained to the loom where he worked. Iqbal didn't laugh or play or go to school, but had to work, instead. He tied tiny knots in wool to make carpets. At the age of ten, with the help of a man working to stop illegal child labor, he gained his freedom. For two years, Iqbal spoke to people around the world about the suffering and injustice experienced by children forced into labor. Because of his boldness in raising awareness about the issue, at twelve years of age, he was murdered.

What Craig read shocked him. He had known nothing of child labor—he didn't even know where Pakistan was—but he soon learned that child labor had grown into a worldwide problem, and he knew he needed to help. Initially, his parents thought of his activism as a phase that Craig would grow out of. Once they realized their son's commitment to helping children in need, they did everything they could to guide and support his mission. In 1995, he gathered eleven school friends and, with them, began speaking out against child labor. He founded Free the Children, which has become the largest network of children-helping-children, through education, in the world. Over the years, Free the Children has built more than 450 schools, implemented clean water programs, delivered medical supplies, and supported healthcare centers around the world. With more than a million child members, its awards and accomplishments number many.

Of course, none of us wishes our children to become martyrs for a cause, as Iqbal did, but we do hope your children will want to start a "movement of kindness" in their communities or even throughout the world, emulating Craig.

Small Changes Make a Big Difference: Ways You Can Better Your Community

How can you and your children start a positive epidemic in your own community? Malcolm Gladwell, author of *The Tipping Point,* suggests that three factors make up the basis of change—what it takes to start an epidemic, or mass change, for the good.[1] First, he maintains that a small number of people tend to take responsibility for most of the work in creating transformation. Economists are familiar with the 80/20 rule, which states that for many experiences, 80 percent of outcomes come from 20 percent of the causes. Gladwell believes it takes even fewer people to tip an epidemic. Witness Candace Lightner and Michael Josephson.

Second, we must see a context for change, an environment conducive to the epidemic we want to create. As parents, we may have the desire to teach our children about giving and caring in their world and, individually, we can take steps to ensure our kids get the message, but we can also illuminate the importance and value of teaching *all* kids to care, by working on our concerns and solutions as a community.

Finally, the message needs to take hold in people's minds. As more parents and leaders believe in the importance of teaching children ways of caring, and strive to model the behavior for them, the significance of the message grows. In the end, most successful positive epidemics start with believing in the possibility of change, and in trusting that people *can* transform beliefs and behaviors based on the right kind of impetus.

Can volitionally teaching kids to care tip a positive epidemic in our communities? We think so. Here are some ways you can make a difference.

Two young volunteers proudly serve the homeless.

Be the Change

Look for ways you and your kids can make connections with groups in your community.

- Contact your Chamber of Commerce or local Community Center to see what environmental needs exist in your city, or organize your own neighborhood or school cleanup.

- Contact a local senior citizen's residence and encourage the able-bodied to get out into the community to work with children. Seniors and children are a natural fit. Organize a reading club at the library, where seniors can read to children. Seniors mentor children in a great many ways.

- Contact your local Head Start office to see how you can bring groups of children to read to or work with younger Head Start children.

- Contact your local Boys and Girls Clubs and get the after-school program to offer a "Make It for Others" program. For example, find out what your local children's hospital may need for its patients, or what will benefit kids in crisis centers. What can children offer other children in need?

- Fire and police departments often raise money or collect toys for burn victims, abused children, and many other people in need. Find out how your school or community group can "adopt" the giving mission of your local public services and help their work make a larger impact. Ask what you and your family can do to participate in their efforts.

Find groups already existing in your community and bring together talent and need. Tapping into already-organized good works can encourage others to get involved and help groups accomplish more together than alone.

Get the Word Out

Too often, we focus on the negative things that happen in our communities and around the world. Create an opportunity to turn toward the positive and promote noteworthy action for kids by getting the good news out!

- Organize and publicize an event to get children out into the community to help. In the age of the Internet, once you identify a need and a plan, you can easily start an e-mail blast to educate, and also invite parents to participate. This not only creates an opportunity for action, but provides a chance to let others learn how they, too, can get involved.

- Work with your child's teacher or principal to hold school-wide or classroom events. Clean the school; plant and care for a community garden; create other projects that help children make an impact on their community or learn more about the needs of others and then publicize it. Encourage your school's staff to promote the need for a school publication that focuses on helping with community projects and other giving opportunities, and spur on the students to create. Show youngsters ways to get involved.

- Adopt a community agency that cares for children, and then raise funds, collect supplies, and make time to give to the children. The supplies might include books, toys, or clothes. And, kids can gather costumes for Halloween or gifts for the holidays.

- Have your kids, or a group of kids, host a party for children in need. Make a piñata or something special to celebrate their connection.

- Set up engagements for local leaders to speak about their relevant community agencies at your child's school or local Boys and Girls Club. They will inspire kids to give their time.

- Through the school paper or flyers to parents, publicize and report on the good works others are doing.

- Learn about your local media. What local publications or TV and radio stations can you contact to spread the word about ways children are making a difference in your community? Make news by organizing such programs, and keep the media informed by sending pictures and articles. Encourage children to participate by writing about their own experiences of giving, and submit them, also.

Note: Kids Korps USA has a monthly spot in its newsletter to report events and kids' stories about their experiences.

Gain Support

There is power in numbers. Organize groups of parents and community gatherings on a regular basis, tap into programs that already exist, or start your own group to create social connections and solutions to controversial issues that face your children and your community. We've listed below some examples of how people come together in positive ways.

- A group of mothers organized Mothers of Boys (MOB) and scheduled monthly meetings to discuss their middle-school and high-school boys' development and needs, and problem-solve the ways to keep them engaged in healthy behaviors as they grow. This kind of group can be organized for boys or girls in your school.

- Circle of Friends (COF) started as a homegrown group of female philanthropists organized to identify community needs for children. Members make individual visits to community agencies and gather information about programs in need of funding. Each woman presents her newly found information to the larger group. COF chooses one organization per year, and the combined funds make a large impact. Start a philanthropic group. More can be accomplished in numbers.

- Bring together like-minded parents and their kids to clean a park, feed the homeless, visit a senior center, or raise funds for a good cause.

- Join a pre-existing organization, such as Kids Korps USA, that offers hundreds of programs to help communities.

- Start a political action group that can identify children's issues in your community.

You can copy these ideas, or come up with your own, but the key is: *do something.* You *can* make a difference!

Know Your Community Leaders

Do you know the political leaders in your community?

Do you know their positions on after-school programs for children, or laws and regulations governing school safety?

Do they support school bonds and other funding for school lunch programs and/or service learning programs?

What are they doing about infrastructure for kids, such as curfew regulations and teen centers?

- In California, Kids Korps USA has worked diligently to develop a relationship with many major organizations and agencies to help develop volunteer programs throughout the state. Look for such opportunities in your own states.

- Get to know your elected congressional officials and where they stand on children's issues. Check out your mayor's record on policies related to children.

- Write letters to express concerns and solutions for children.

- Make calls to public offices to share your position on issues.

- Organize others to share a group voice. Parents often have a position, which you can voice through your elected officials.

- Contact the presidents or leaders of your local PTA, Junior League, Rotary Club, Girl Scouts, Boy Scouts, Boys and Girls Clubs, YMCA, or other groups that advocate for children, and find out how they work in the community. Be a catalyst for combining community need with helping organizations.

Your voice matters. When your elected officials and leaders, who work on behalf of children, come to know you as a parent—interested, concerned, and noting any progress toward supporting children—you have engaged in the first step of community change. We all, children and adults alike, want to feel useful. Taking action as an energetic member in your community builds feelings of goodness and usefulness. Through action, you can establish a wave of caring.

Opening ourselves to serving others in our families gives us a stronger sense of purpose, and when we bring this same energy to our communities, it creates a spiral of positive growth and wellness. Small projects, started on an individual basis, can engender grassroots efforts that positively affect other families, the community, and an even broader social base. Change happens from within. When we make the effort to change things for the better, we inspire those around us to do the same. The ripple you and your kids can make with just one outreach will have enduring effects you can measure, both through how you feel about the good you've done and the positive results you will feel in the world around you.

A youth volunteer assists in a therapeutic riding program for children with physical and mental disabilities.

Through the five touchstones of *Teaching Kids to Care,* the ideas of finding meaning and living a purposeful life come to the fore. Of course, most young children don't feel inclined to think about the purpose and meaning of their lives. And as children mature into young adults, they may—or may not—begin asking "big" life questions. But evidence—and our own experience—points to a relationship between giving, meaning, and greater life satisfaction. So, this mandates teaching children—from an early age—how to appreciate what they have, how to be depended on, how to depend on others, how to befriend, how to see and appreciate differences, and how to cultivate joy. They may not comprehend the value of these touchstones at first, but these qualities, more often than not, will breed the competence, compassion, and character we hope our children will develop as they grow.

Strong positive relationships and strong positive communities don't just happen; we create and sustain them through vision, focus, and effort. The five touchstones can help give rise to more individual and social vitality by connecting us to the importance of our value to one another.

The more we spend time getting to know and caring about others, whether as a family or as a community, the richer our lives. A well-worn path from the early sages and philosophers to modern sociologists and neuroscientists suggests that the way to joy, contentment, and mental health entails the taking of interest in, and caring for, others. Everyone has abilities and ways of making a difference, and what better time than now to make use of these gifts?

THE CALL

These little people . . . and big . . .
children and teens . . .
hear the call:
"Come and help."
"Pitch in."
"Give a hand."

It's deep inside somewhere, this call,
in their hearts, in their souls;
So, they come
to give,
to share,
to serve.

They come as one . . . or two . . .
and become a team
and become a Korps,
a Kids Korps.

The real growth, though, is inside
when each child, each teen
feels their hearts grow large with love.

They've learned to care
and it feels so right, so good, so true.
These angels in kids' clothing—
big smiles . . .
big hugs . . .
big hearts.

—Charlie Lehman

Epilogue

We hope this book will inspire you to teach your children the many ways they can care for others while developing competence, character, and compassion. Imagine your kids gaining a healthy perspective on life, understanding the importance of interdependence, connecting with others at school and in the community, feeling grateful for all they have, and getting inspired to make a difference—as they become our next generation of leaders. You will be amazed how teaching kids to care for others innately envelops the five touchstones and creates wonderful life-altering experiences your kids will remember forever.

Can kids get hooked on service? Absolutely!

Kids Korps' mission is to teach kids to care and to provide valuable education in leadership and responsibility.

Would you like your kids to become Kids Korps members?

Are there service projects you'd like to suggest?

To learn more about Kids Korps and whether or not it is in your community, or to volunteer and become a part of this exciting youth volunteer organization, go to www.kidskorps.org.

We are committed to "Teaching Kids to Care" and providing today's youth with service opportunities through Kids Korps USA. If you want additional information about Kids Korps USA or if you would like to invite us to speak at your group's meeting or at an upcoming state, regional, or national conference, send us an email at: www.kidskorps.org.

Kids Korps USA National Headquarters
265 Santa Helena, Suite 130
Solana Beach, CA 92075
Ph: 858-259-3602
Fax: 858-259-3603

Kids Korps USA

Appendix A
Resources for Teaching Kids to Care

An asterisk (*) indicates umbrella organizations that list several volunteer agencies.

America's Promise: www.americaspromise.org
America's Promise—The Alliance for Youth, led by General Colin Powell, is dedicated to mobilizing individuals, groups, and organizations from every part of American life to build and strengthen the character and competence of our youth.

Citizen Corps: www.citizencorps.gov
This initiative supports volunteer service by engaging individuals in promoting the safety of our communities. Through Citizen Corps Councils, the program brings together leaders from law enforcement, fire, emergency medical and other emergency management, volunteer organizations, local elected officials, and the private sector to help them coordinate and engage citizens in homeland security and promote community and family safety.

*The Corporation for National Service:
www.nationalservice.org
The Corporation for National and Community Service was formed

to engage Americans of all ages and backgrounds in service to meet community needs. Each year, more than 1.5 million individuals of all ages and backgrounds help meet local needs through a wide array of service opportunities. These include projects in education, the environment, public safety, homeland security, and other critical areas through the Corporation's three major programs: Senior Corps, AmeriCorps, and Learn and Serve America.

The Fuller Center for Housing: www.fullercenter.org
The Fuller Center for Housing is a nonprofit, ecumenical Christian housing ministry dedicated to eliminating substandard housing and homelessness worldwide and to making adequate, affordable shelter a matter of conscience and action. The Fuller Center for Housing invites people from all faiths and walks of life to work together in partnership, building houses with families in need. The Fuller Center for Housing is founded by Millard and Linda Fuller, founders of Habitat for Humanity.

Hands On Network: www.handsonnetwork.org
Hands On Network (formerly CityCares) is a growing, innovative alliance of volunteer mobilization and management organizations providing best practices, leading-edge programs, influence in national service policy, technology support, and leadership development. Hands On Network organizations around the world are transforming people and communities through volunteer service and civic engagement.

JustGive: www.justgive.org
JustGive is a nonprofit organization whose mission is to connect people with the charities and causes they care about and to increase overall giving. There is a coalition of leading nonprofits, foundations, and corporations encouraging us to "Give Five"—

donate 5 percent of our income and volunteer five hours a week.

Kids Korps USA: www.kidskorps.org
Kids Korps USA is a nonprofit youth volunteer organization that engages young people, ages five through eighteen, in community service. They instill in America's youth the spirit of giving while providing valuable education in leadership and responsibility. They provide hands-on service to national and local nonprofits such as Special Olympics, women's resource centers, homeless shelters, children's hospitals, senior centers, and environmental projects.

Learn and Serve America: www.learnandserve.org or www.learnandserve.gov
Learn and Serve America is at the forefront of the service learning movement, linking classroom instruction with community service.

Points of Light Foundation: www.pointsoflight.org
The Points of Light Foundation, based in Washington, DC, advocates community service through a partnership with the Volunteer Center National Network (www.1-800-volunteer.org). Together, they reach millions of people in thousands of communities to help mobilize people and resources, which deliver solutions that address community problems. The Foundation's mission is to engage more people and resources more effectively in volunteer service to help solve serious social problems.

Roots and Shoots: www.janegoodall.org
Roots and Shoots is a nationwide network of children working for environmental and humanitarian efforts. It is a project of the Jane Goodall Institute.

Teach for America: www.teachforamerica.org
Teach for America (TFA), a nonprofit organization, recruits primarily recent college graduates of all academic majors to teach for two years in an under-resourced urban or rural public school; however, they welcome applicants at all age and experience levels. If you've ever considered the idea of teaching others what you have learned, you might want to look more closely at this opportunity. Certification not required.

*USA Freedom Corps Volunteer Network:
www.usafreedomcorps.gov
The USA Freedom Corps Volunteer Network is the most comprehensive clearinghouse of volunteer opportunities ever created. For the first time in history, Americans can enter geographic information about where they want to get involved, such as state or zip code, and areas of interest ranging from education to the environment, to access volunteer opportunities offered by a range of partner organizations across the country and around the world.

*VolunteerMatch: www.volunteermatch.org
VolunteerMatch is "dedicated to helping everyone find a great place to volunteer." Interested volunteers can enter their zip code on the website home page to quickly find local volunteer opportunities posted by nonprofit organizations throughout the United States.

Youth Service America: www.ysa.org
Youth Service America works through an alliance of more than 300 organizations committed to increasing opportunities for young Americans to serve. Youth Service America's SERVEnet is an online service and resource center that links volunteers of all

ages to causes in their communities. Users enter their zip code, city, skills, interests, and availability, to match up with organizations that need help from young people.

As a family, you can take action in your community. You can rally your family, friends, or school to do something that reaches out and benefits others. The power of service comes from knowing that what you do matters, so move forward to connect your kids to their efforts from beginning a project to experiencing the impact on others.

Letters and Care Packages for the Military:
Volunteers are always wanted to write letters for American troops overseas. Bundle together group letters and cards and send in one large envelope or box. Troops also want used or new DVDs for entertainment. Check the following websites:
www.anysoldier.com
www.operationinterdependence.org
www.forgottensoldiers.org

We Care Packages for Meals On Wheels:
During the holidays and for every birthday, Meals On Wheels and a community of generous volunteers provide seniors with a special goodie bag to say, "We Care." Small gifts will fit nicely into brightly covered shoeboxes or decorated paper shopping bags. Assemble We Care Packages with a male or female in mind and include a personal note of well wishes from students or volunteers. Suggested items: snack size or individually wrapped food items such as nuts, oatmeal, granola bars, and applesauce, personal care items (toothbrushes, shampoo, Kleenex), convenience goods (socks and dish towels), Post-it notes. Contact your local Meals On Wheels program.

Head Start Preschool Shoebox Project:
Cover a shoebox with wrapping paper and fill with one of each of the following for preschool-age children: toiletry, toy, hat, mittens, and book. Contact your local Head Start program.

Adopt/Support Someone Fighting Cancer:
Add a ray of sunshine to someone who is undergoing treatment for cancer. Provide emotional support and bring a smile to your personally assigned patient by sending one to two cards and/or gifts per week during the most challenging time of their lives. This can be done by an individual, a family, or even on a rotated basis through a group. Gifts need not be expensive, but just consistent. For all the details and volunteer applications go to www.chemoangels.net.

Make A Child Smile:
Each month, www.makeachildsmile.com features three children with life-threatening illnesses. The goal: for these children to receive hundreds of warm wishes through cards and thoughts of love (either handmade or commercially printed). The parents of these children appreciate this support as much as the kids do. Visit the website to get the bios and addresses of the kids. Provide this service on a one-time-only basis, or even once a month, for each of the featured children. (The site is updated on the first of each month.) Great project for a group to work on together!

Keiki Cards:
Have an art party and make dozens of cards for terminally ill children. Keiki Cards provides envelopes for cards up to 4¼ inches by 5½ inches. Include a happy message such as "Thinking of You," "Hi!", "You're Great!", "Have a Happy Day!" But do not say "Get Well" (since most of these children have terminal illnesses), and do not include religious messages. Separate cards for boys and girls, and mark them accordingly. Flat gifts such as stickers, bookmarks,

and origami are also welcome, as are postage-stamp donations. Send everything all together to Keiki Cards, PMB 5-532, 4224 Waialea Ave., Honolulu, HI 96816 or go to www.keikicards.org for more details. This group will then remail your contributions to in-need children from their national database.

Tray Liners:
Create meal-tray liners to use when serving the elderly or needy. Decorate them in festive ways, and with friendly and uplifting messages. And, your local Salvation Army appreciates receiving decorative trays. You may want to contact them.

Charity Chest:
Set a box aside for things and put stuff in it that you don't want, as you come across these items. Having it out in the open will be a constant reminder to you to donate to others and help keep your life free of clutter. When the chest gets full, have a family meeting and collectively decide to which agencies you would like to donate the items.

Recommended Children's Books and Tapes with Themes of Giving

The Giving Book: Open the Door to a Lifetime of Giving, by Ellen Sabin (Watering Can Press, 2004). "When you care about things that nurture them, they will grow healthy; strong; and happy; and, in turn, will make the world a better place."

Giving Thanks: A Native American Good Morning Message, by Chief Jake Swamp (Lee & Low Books, 1995). This picture book's text is based on the Thanksgiving Address: "an ancient message of peace and appreciation of Mother Earth and all her inhabitants" from the Iroquois. Acrylic paintings on canvas by Erwin Printup Jr. strikingly capture the beauty of nature with drama and simplicity. A book the entire family will appreciate.

The Giving Tree, by Shel Silverstein (Evil Eye Music, 1964). This book teaches that we can ultimately feel satisfied by the gifts we give, independent of how others appreciate them.

Hooray for You: A Celebration of You-ness, by Marianne Richmond (Waldman House Press, 2001). This book helps young children accept who they are.

In Every Tiny Grain of Sand: A Child's Book of Prayers and Praise, by Reeve Lindbergh (Candlewick Press, 2000). The author divided this book into four sections: For the Day, For the Home, For the Earth, and For the Night—each with a different illustrator, with selections from a variety of authors, cultures, and religions. You will delight in the wonderful illustrations and meaningful selections. The book's emphasis is on giving thanks and it is written to be enjoyed by all ages.

Kids' Random Acts of Kindness, edited by Dawna Markova (Conari Press, 1994). Heartwarming stories of good deeds.

Miss Rumphius, by Barbara Cooney (Scholastic, 1985). Miss Rumphius leaves the world a better place by scattering lupine seeds everywhere she goes and leaving a legacy of blue flowers. She sets an example for her niece.

The Rainbow Fish, by Marcus Pfister (North-South Books, 1992). The story suggests that even though the rewards of vanity appear grand, they will never compare with the true joy of selfless giving.

Stone Soup. One of many renditions. Reluctant villagers end up sharing precious food resources with hungry strangers. With the help of the clever strangers, the whole village comes together to make a delicious soup no individual could have made alone— soup that started with just stones.

Audiotapes

Movies of My Mind Adventures (Imagination Development Group, 2004). An audio series that offers children "movies without pictures" to stimulate their imaginations. The stories in it focus on people in history who had strong characters, such as Amelia Earhart (aviation pioneer), Wilma Rudolph (Olympic gold medalist), Valentina Tereshkova (first woman in space), and Tenzing Norgay and Edmund Hillary (first men to climb Mount Everest).

In Harmony: A Sesame Street Record (Warner Brothers Records, 1980). An old recording, but a gem. It presents songs for children by well-known artists. Some featured tunes: "Be with Me" by Carly Simon, "One Good Turn" by Al Jarreau, "A Friend for All Seasons" by George Benson, and "In Harmony" by Kate Taylor.

Websites That Inspire Compassion, Competence, and Character

Character Counts!: www.charactercounts.org
provides extensive training programs and a wide range of age-appropriate teaching aids for parents and character educators.

Charity Focus: www.charityfocus.org
offers inspiration for those who focus on giving to others, including daily quotes.

Free the Children: www.freethechildren.org
the world's largest network of children helping children through education. The organization's unique youth-driven approach involves more than one million young people in innovative programs and spans more than forty-five countries.

The Josephson Institute of Ethics:
www.josephsoninstitute.org
founded to improve the ethical quality of society by changing personal and organizational decision-making and behavior, the institute created and runs Character Counts!; the Pursuing Victory with Honor sportsmanship campaign; Foundations for Life; and other projects. The institute is a nonpartisan and nonsectarian 501(c)(3) nonprofit organization.

The Random Acts of Kindness Foundation:
www.actsofkindness.org
offers ideas for sharing kindness with others.

Appendix B
Suggested Reading

Ban Breathnach, Sarah. *Simple Abundance: A Daybook of Comfort and Joy.* New York: Warner Books, 1995.

Bellah, Robert, Richard Madsen, William Sullivan, Ann Swidler, and Steven Tipton. *Habits of the Heart.* Berkeley, CA: University of California Press, 1985.

Benson, Peter L. *All Kids Are Our Kids.* San Francisco: Jossey-Bass, 1997.

Benson, Peter L., Judy Galbraith, and Pamela Espeland. *What Kids Need to Succeed.* Minneapolis: Free Spirit, 1998.

Butterworth, Eric. *Discover the Power within You.* San Francisco: HarperSanFrancisco, 1992.

Chapman, Gary, and Ross Campbell. *The Five Love Languages of Children.* Chicago: Moody Press, 1997.

Chopra, Deepak. *The Path to Love: Renewing the Power of Spirit in Your Life.* New York: Harmony Books, 1997.

———. *The Seven Spiritual Laws for Parents: Guiding Your Children to Success and Fulfillment.* New York: Harmony Books, 1997.

Coles, Robert. *The Call of Service: A Witness to Idealism.* Boston: Houghton Mifflin, 1993.

Covey, Sean. *The 7 Habits of Highly Effective Teens.* New York: Simon & Schuster, 1998.

Craig, Jenny. *The Jenny Craig Story: How One Woman Changes Millions of Lives.* Hoboken, NJ: John Wiley & Sons, 2004.

Csikszentmihalyi, Mihaly. *Flow: The Psychology of Optimal Experience.* New York: Harper & Row, 1990.

DeGraaf, John, David Wann, and Thomas H. Naylor. *Affluenza: The All Consuming Epidemic.* San Francisco: Berrett-Koehler, 2001.

Desetta, Al, and Sybil Wolin. *The Struggle to Be Strong.* Minneapolis: Free Spirit, 2000.

Diotte, Manuel. *Happiness Is a Pair of Shorts.* San Antonio, TX: Dare to Dream, 2002.

Edelman, Marian. *The Measure of Our Success.* New York: HarperCollins, 1992.

Edwards, Bob, Michael W. Foley, and Mario Diani. *Beyond Tocqueville.* Hanover, NH: University Press of New England, 2001.

Egan, Hope. *Volunteering.* New York: Silver Lining Books, 2002.

Eisler, Riane. *Tomorrow's Children.* Boulder, CO: Westview Press, 2000.

Espeland, Pamela. *Succeed Every Day—Daily Readings for Teens.* Minneapolis: Free Spirit, 2001.

Freedman, Bryn, and William Knoedelseder. *In Eddie's Name.* New York: Faber and Faber, 1999.

Friedman, Thomas L. *The World Is Flat.* New York: Farrar, Straus and Giroux, 2005.

Glenn, H. Stephen, and Jane Nelsen. *Raising Self-Reliant Children in a Self-Indulgent World.* Rocklin, CA: Prima, 1989.

Goleman, Daniel. *Emotional Intelligence.* New York: Bantam, 1995.

Goodall, Jane, with Phillip Berman. *Reason for Hope: A Spiritual Journey.* New York: Warner Books, 1999.

Green, Bob. *Once Upon a Town.* New York: William Morrow, 2002.

Greer, Colin, and Herbert Kohl. *A Call to Character.* New York: HarperCollins, 1995.

Heim, Susan M. *It's Twins! Parent-to-Parent Advice from Infancy Through Adolescence.* Charlottesville, VA: Hampton Roads, 2007.

Kasich, John. *Stand for Something: The Battle for America's Soul.* New York: Warner Books, 2006.

Kehoe, John. *The Practice of Happiness.* Vancouver, BC: Zoetic, 1999.

Kilpatrick, Joseph, and Sanford Danziger (compilers). *Better Than Money Can Buy.* Winston-Salem, NC: Innersearch, 1996.

Kilpatrick, William, and Gregory and Suzanne M. Wolfe. *Books That Build Character.* New York: Simon & Schuster, 1994.

Layard, Richard. *Happiness: Lessons from a New Science.* New York: Penguin, 2005.

Lewis, Barbara. *The Kid's Guide to Service Projects.* Minneapolis: Free Spirit, 1995.

———. *Kids with Courage.* Minneapolis: Free Spirit, 1992.

———. *What Do You Stand For?* Minneapolis: Free Spirit, 1998.

Lewis, Hunter. *A Question of Values.* San Francisco: Harper & Row, 1990.

Mauss, Marcel. *The Gift: The Form and Reason for Exchange in Archaic Societies.* New York: WW Norton, 1990.

Mayeroff, Milton. *On Caring.* New York: Harper & Row, 1971.

McCain, John, and Mark Salter. *Character Is Destiny.* New York: Random House, 2005.

Metzler, Barbara R.. *Passionaries: Turning Compassion into Action.* Philadelphia: Templeton Foundation Press, 2006.

Moore, Thomas. *Care of the Soul.* New York: HarperCollins, 1992.

Morsch, Gary, and Dean Nelson. *The Power of Serving Others.* San Francisco: Berrett-Koehler, 2006.

Nelsen, Jane. *Positive Discipline.* New York: Ballantine, 1981.

Nelson, Alan, and Stan Toler. *The 5 Secrets to Becoming a Leader.* Ventura, CA: Regal, 2002.

Northrup, Christine. *Mother-Daughter Wisdom.* New York: Bantam, 2005.

Papalia, Diane E., and Sally Wendkos Olds. *Human Development* (Seventh Edition). New York: McGraw-Hill, 1998.

Phelan, Thomas W. *Self-Esteem Revolutions in Children.* Glen Ellyn, IL: Child Management, 1996.

Piaget, Jean. *The Moral Judgment of the Child.* New York: Free Press, 1997.

Popkin, Michael, PhD. *Active Parenting Now.* Atlanta, GA: Active Parenting, 2002.

———. *Taming the Spirited Child: Strategies for Parenting Challenging Children without Breaking Their Spirits.* New York: Fireside/Simon & Schuster, 2007.

Price, Susan Crites. *The Giving Family.* Washington, DC: Council on Foundations, 2005.

Putnam, Robert D. *Bowling Alone: The Collapse and Revival of American Community.* New York: Simon & Schuster, 2000.

Rusch, Elizabeth. *Generation Fix.* Hillsboro, OR: Beyond Words, 2002.

Ryan, M.J. *Attitudes of Gratitude.* Berkeley, CA: Conari Press, 1999.

Stuart, Timothy S., and Cheryl G. Bostrom. *Children at Promise.* San Francisco: Jossey-Bass, 2003.

Summers, Diane. *Parenting outside the Box.* Fallbrook, CA: Summerville Spirit, 2006.

Tofler, Ian, and Theresa Foy DiGeronimo. *Keeping Your Kids Out Front without Kicking Them from Behind.* San Francisco: Jossey-Bass, 2000.

Vardey, Lucinda. *A Simple Path: Mother Teresa.* New York: Ballantine, 1995.

Waldman, Jackie. *Teens with the Courage to Give.* Berkeley, CA: Conari Press, 2000.

Weisman, Carol. *Raising Charitable Children.* St. Louis, MO: FE Robbins & Sons, 2006.

Wuthnow, Robert. *Learning to Care.* New York: Oxford University Press, 1995.

Youngs, Bettie B., EdD, PhD. *Gifts of the Heart.* Deerfield Beach, FL: Health Communications, 1999.

———. *The House That Love Built: The Story of Millard and Linda Fuller, Founders of Habitat for Humanity and the Fuller Center for Housing.* Charlottesville, VA: Hampton Roads Publishing, 2007.

———. *How to Develop Self-Esteem in Your Child.* New York: Random House, 1999.

———. *Problem Solving Skills for Children.* Austin, TX: Jalmar Press, 2000.

———. *Safeguarding Your Teenager from the Dragons of Life.* Deerfield Beach, FL: Health Communications, 1998.

———. *Stress & Your Child: Helping Kids Cope with the Strains & Pressures of Life.* New York: Random House, 1998.

———. *Taste-Berry Tales: Stories to Lift the Spirit, Fill the Heart and Feed the Soul.* Deerfield Beach, FL: Health Communications, 1999.

Youngs, Bettie, Linda C. Fuller, and Donna M. Schuller. *Woman to Woman Wisdom: Inspiration for REAL Life.* Nashville, TN: Thomas Nelson, 2005.

Youngs, Bettie, and Masa Goetz, PhD. *Getting Back Together: How to Reconcile with Your Partner, and Make It Last* (Second Edition). Avon, MA: Adams Media, 2006.

Youngs, Bettie, and Jane Healy. *Parents on Board: Building Academic Success through Parent Involvement* (leader's guide). Atlanta, GA: Active Parenting, 1999.

Youngs, Bettie, Susan M. Heim, and Jennifer L. Youngs. *Oh, Baby! 7 Ways a Baby Will Change Your Life in the First Year.* Charlottesville, VA: Hampton Roads, 2006.

Youngs, Bettie, Michael Popkin, PhD., and Jane Healy. *Helping Your Child Succeed in School.* Marietta, GA: Active Parenting, 2000.

———. *Parents on Board: Building Academic Success through Parent Involvement* (video-based program). Atlanta, GA: Active Parenting, 1999.

Youngs, Bettie B., EdD, PhD., and Jennifer Leigh Youngs. *365 Days of Taste-Berry Inspiration for Teens.* Deerfield Beach, FL: Health Communications, 2003.

———. *The Moments & Milestones Pregnancy Journal: A Week-by-Week Companion.* New York: Amacom, 2006.

———. *More Taste Berries for Teens: A Second Collection of Short Stories and Encouragement on Life, Love, Friendship and Tough Issues.* Deerfield Beach, FL: Health Communications, 2000.

———. *Taste Berries for Teens: Inspirational Short Stories and Encouragement on Life, Love, Friendship and Tough Issues.* Deerfield Beach, FL: Health Communications, 1999.

———. *Taste Berries for Teens #3: Inspirational Short Stories on Life, Love, Friends and the Face in the Mirror.* Deerfield Beach, FL: Health Communications, 2002.

———. *Taste Berries for Teens #4: Inspirational Short Stories on Being Cool, Caring and Courageous.* Deerfield Beach, FL: Health Communications, 2004.

———. *Taste Berries for Teens Journal: My Thoughts on Life, Love and Making a Difference.* Deerfield Beach, FL: Health Communications, 2000.

———. *A Taste-Berry Teen's Guide to Managing the Stress and Pressures of Life.* Deerfield Beach, FL: Health Communications, 2001.

————. *A Taste-Berry Teen's Guide to Setting and Achieving Goals.* Deerfield Beach, FL: Health Communications, 2002.

————. *A Teen's Guide to Living Drug-Free.* Deerfield Beach, FL: Health Communications, 2003.

Youngs, Jennifer Leigh. *Feeling Great, Looking Hot and Loving Yourself: Health, Fitness & Beauty for Teens.* Deerfield Beach, FL: Health Communications, 2000.

Zink, Dr. J. *Champions in the Making.* Atlanta: Peregrinzilla Press, 1995.

————. *Upbringing: Raising Emotionally Intelligent Children.* Atlanta: Peregrinzilla Press, 1997.

Endnotes

Chapter 1

1. Bryn Freedman and William Knoedelseder. *In Eddie's Name*. New York: Faber and Faber, 1999.

2. Ibid.

3. Adapted from Diane Papala and Sally Wendokos Olds. *Human Development* (Seventh Edition). New York: McGraw-Hill, 1998, pp. 238–239; and Diana Baumrind. "Effects of Authoritative Parental Control on Child Behavior." *Child Development,* December 1966, Vol. 37, No. 4, pp. 887–907.

4. Victoria J. Rideout, Donald Roberts, and Ulla Foehr. *Generation M: Media in the Lives of 8–18-Year-Olds*, A Kaiser Family Foundation Survey, March 9, 2005.

5. Victoria J. Rideout, Elizabeth A. Vanderwater, and Ellen A. Wartella. *Zero to Six: The Henry J. Kaiser Family Foundation Study,* Fall 2003.

6. *Key Facts.* The Kaiser Family Foundation, Spring 2003.

7. Albert Bandura, D. Ross, and S. A. Ross. "Transmission of Aggression through Imitation of Aggressive Models." *Journal of Abnormal and Social Psychology,* 1961; 63:575–582.

8. Albert Bandura, D. Ross, and S. A. Ross. "Imitation of Film-Mediated Aggressive Models." *Journal of Abnormal and Social Psychology*, 1963, 66.

9. *The Ethics of American Youth: 2006 Report Card*, Josephson Institute of Ethics, October 15, 2006.

Chapter 2

1. David McClelland. "The Effect of Motivational Arousal through Films on Salivary Immunoglobulin A." *Psychological Health* 1988; 2:31–52.
2. Sonja Lyubomirsky. *Professional Profile.* University of California, Riverside, January 6, 2006.
3. Hans Selye. *The Stress of Life.* New York: McGraw-Hill, 1956. Excerpted from *Kindness: How Good Deeds Can Be Good for You.* Random Acts of Kindness Foundation, 2004.
4. Lisa F. Berkman and S. Leonard Syme. "Social Networks, Host Resistance, and Mortality: A Nine-Year Follow-Up Study of Alameda County Residents." *American Journal of Epidemiology* 1979; 109:186–204.
5. K. Miller, S. Schleien, S. Schlemiel, D. Lehman. "Teaming Up for Inclusive Volunteering," *Loisir,* Fall 2003.

Chapter 4

1. Adapted from Diane Papalia and Sally Wendkos Olds. *Human Development, Seventh Edition.* Boston, Massachusetts: McGraw-Hill, 1998, pp. 352–353.

Chapter 5

1. Tina Kapinos. "'Popular' Kids Not Always Nice," *Chicago Tribune,* August 16, 2006.
2. *Hardwired to Connect: The New Scientific Case for Authoritative Communities.* A Report to the Nation from the Commission on Children at Risk. Institute for American Values, 2003.
3. Robert Putnam. "You Gotta Have Friends," *Time,* June 25, 2006.
4. Naomi Eisenberger, M. D. Lieberman, K. D. Williams. "Does Rejection Hurt? An MRI Study of Social Exclusion." *Science.* October 2003; 302:290–292.

Chapter 6

1. *Teenage Brain: A Work in Progress,* National Institute of Mental Health, 2001.
2. Lucinda M. Wilson and Hadley Wilson Horch. "Implications of Brain Research for Teaching Young Adolescents," *Middle School Journal* 2002; 34(1):57–61.

Chapter 7

1. Robert A. Emmons and Michael E. McCullough. "Counting Blessings versus Burdens: An Experimental Investigation of Gratitude and Subjective Well-Being in Daily Life." *Journal of Personality and Social Psychology* 2003; 84:377–389.
2. Sam Quick and A. Lesueur. *Benefits of Gratitude.* University of Kentucky Cooperative Extension Service, 2003.
3. Monica Y. Bartlett and David DeSteno. "Gratitude and Prosocial Behavior: Helping When It Costs You." *Psychological Science* 2006; 17:319–325.
4. Robert A. Emmons and Michael E. McCullough. "Highlights from the Research Project on Gratitude and Thankfulness." *Dimensions and Perspectives of Gratitude.*

Chapter 8

1. Walsh, David. *NO: Why Kids of All Ages Need to Hear It and Ways Parents Can Say It.* From Martha Irvine, "U.S. Youths' Priority: Strike It Rich," *Chicago Tribune,* January 23, 2007.
2. Brandt, Ron. "Punished by Rewards? A Conversation with Alfie Kohn." *Educational Leadership,* 1995; 53(1).

Chapter 10

1. Corporation for National Community Service, Independent Sector, and U.S. Census Bureau Issue Brief: "Youth Helping America: The Role of Social Institutions in Teen Volunteering," November, 2005.

Chapter 11

1. Malcolm Gladwell. *The Tipping Point: How Little Things Can Make a Big Difference.* New York: Little, Brown and Company, 2000.

Index

A

abilities, belief in, 40
adventure, sense of, 118
aggressive behavior, 11, 12, 57
    vs. nonaggressive behavior experiment, 11
altruistic egoism, 18
American Academy of Pediatrics, 10
Angela and Arianna's inspirational story, 139–141
antisocial behavior, 11
appreciation. *See* gratitude
"appreciation location," 102
authoritative parenting style, 7

B

Bandura, Albert, 11
"Bare Whitewashed Walls" (inspirational story), 142–144
Baumrind, Diana, 7
Berkman, Lisa, 18
Bobo Doll study, 11
bonding, 55–56, 59
    mental/behavioral problems and, 59
    relationships and, good, 68
    teaching methods on, 63–65
    trustworthy relationships and, developing, 55–56
boundaries, firm, 16
Bowling Alone, 59
"Bowling with Love" (inspirational story), 139–141
"A Boy Name Arturo" (inspirational story), 141–142
Boys and Girls Club, 158, 164, 165
brain, effects of television on, 10–11

C

"The Call" (poem), 180
caring research, importance of, 17–18

"Carving My Name" (inspirational story), 136–137
Casa de Ampara Project, 131–132
change, factors that make up the basis of, 172–173
character, building a sound (good), 13
Character Counts Coalition, 13
Chris's inspirational story, 133–134
Christina's inspirational story, 134–135
Circle of Friends (COF) group, 176
Columbine High School shooting, 57–58
Commission of Children at Risk, 59
communication, 20
community(ies)
    advocates, 165
    Corporation for National and Community Service, 167
    respect for, interdependence and, 28
    safe, 16
    service, 28, 85
compassion
    inspiration and, 116
    life influences and, parental teaching of, 16
    parenting and, key to good, 13
    perspective and, 82, 83
competence, 13, 16, 21, 27
computer technology, 10, 11
confidence, 21
connectedness, types of, 69
connection
    conversation starters for parents about, 71–72
    dangerous influences and, 57
    importance of, 58
    key benefits of, 61–62
    leaders for life and, seven critical steps for developing, 166
    making, part of everyday life and, 68–71
    social adjustment questionnaire, 67–68
    types of, 59
    See also bonding
core values, 28–30
Costner, Kevin, 154

D

Dawn's inspirational story, 136–137
Diana's inspirational story, 146–147
Diotte, Manny, 97
disabled and nondisabled volunteer program study, 18–19

E

electronic media, 10
Elliott's inspirational story, 146

Emotional Intelligence, 62
external rewards, 115–116

F

family connections, 65
Field of Dreams, 154, 156
"Filling Stomachs and Touching Hearts" (inspirational story), 136–137, 137–138
"Flowers to Remember" (inspirational story), 144–146
fortitude, internal, 9
Free the Children movement, 171–172
friendships, deeper, 62

G

generosity, 97
Giedd, Jay, 79
Gladwell, Malcolm, 172
Goleman, Daniel, 62
grateful heart, nurturing, 164
gratitude
    benefits of, key, 96–98
    conversation starters and, 109–111
    everyday life and, 107–109
    experiencing and expressing, four ways to help, 102–103
    expression of, defined, 94
    importance of, 95
    kindness and, acting and reacting with, 17
    leaders for life and, seven critical steps for developing, 166
    levels of, 104–105
    teaching and, 95–96
    thankful life questionnaire and, 106–107

H

Habitat for Humanity, 19
hands-off parenting style, 7–8
happiness
    benefits of, 17
    deeper sense of, 61
Happiness Is a Pair of Shorts, 97
Harris, Eric, 58
healthy perspective, 81
"helicopter parents," 8
"hole in the moral zone," 13
Home Depot, 131–132, 165
hopefulness, 96
hugs, 16
humanitarianism, 63–64

I

"I Wished upon a Shooting Star" (inspirational story), 146
identity, 63
"Imagine a Room Like This" (inspirational story), 134–135
inspiration
    benefits of, key, 117–119
    conversation starters and, 126–127
    defined, 114
    discovering, 116
    everyday life and, 123–126
    internal well of, 117
    kindness and, act and react with, 17
    leaders for life and, seven critical steps for developing, 166
    parental goals and, 115
    questionnaire, 122–123
    "romance of life" and, 116
    spirit of, five ways to instill, 119–121
    See also compassion; Kids Korps USA
interdependence
    benefits of, key, 40–41
    conversation starters and, 50
    everyday lives and, 47–49
    importance of, 21, 164
    Kids Korps USA and, 40, 45
    kindness and, acting and reacting with, 16
    leaders for life and, seven critical steps for developing, 166
    positive and negative aspects of, 33
    questionnaire, 46–47
    spirit of, instilling, 43–44
internal pivotal point, 76
introvert *vs.* extrovert, 65

J

Jarred's inspirational story, 142–144
Josephson, Michael, 13, 170, 171, 172
Josephson Institute of Ethics, 13
joy, spontaneous, 97

K

Kids Korps USA
    Casa de Ampara Project and, 131–132
    core values of, 28–30
    giving and, habit of the heart and, 159–162
    inspiration and, 117
    inspiring testimonies from, 133–151
    interdependence and, 40, 45
    kids of, incredible, 162–164

leaders of, three testimonials from, 146–151
mission of, 158–159
perspective and, 79
purpose of the organization, 20–22
values of, 164–166
vision of, 154–158
volunteerism and, 166–167
Kielburger, Craig, 171
kindness, hugs, and kisses, 16
Kirshnit, Carol, 17
kisses, 16
Klebold, Dylan, 57–58
Kohlberg, Lawrence, 38
Kohlberg's stages of moral development, 38–39
Kohn, Alfie, 115
Kristen's inspirational story, 133
Kyle's inspirational story, 141–142

L

latchkey kids, 57
leader *vs.* follower, 66
leaders, next generation, 17
leaders for life, seven critical steps for developing, 166
leadership, 41
Leeann's inspirational story, 147–148
Lehman, Charlie, 180
Lehman, Dawn, 18, 156
life direction, 118
Lightner, Candace, 170, 171, 172
listening skills, modeling good, 86
Little Engine That Could, 66
Lyubormirsky, Sonja, 17

M

Masih, Iqbal, 171
McClelland, David, 17
media and moral-bending images, influences of, 10–12
mentoring, 164
The Miracle Worker, 66
models, volunteer, 165
moral bending images, 11
moral development, stages of, 38–39
moral fiber, strengthening, 13
morality
    conventional, 38
    premoral/preconventional, 38
Mothers Against Drunk Driving (MADD), 170
Mothers of Boys (MOB) group, 176

motivation, intrinsic, 115
music venues, 10

N

NO: Why Kids of All Ages Need to Hear It and Ways Parents Can Say It, 115
nonaggressive behavior, 11

O

obesity, 10
objective perspective, 82
optimism, 82, 96
optimist *vs.* pessimist, 66
outward pivotal point, 76
overindulgence, 8–9
over-involved parenting style, 7, 8

P

paradigm examination, 84
parenting
    authoritative style of, 7
    compassion and
        as key to, 13
        life influences and, parental teaching of, 16
    connection and, conversation starters about, 71–72
    doing too much or too little and, 6–9
    hands-off style of, 7–8
    "helicopter parents" and, 8
    inspiration and, goals of, 115
    over-involved style of, 7, 8
    permissive style of, 7
    raising kids who care, good skills as key to, 12–13
    techniques of, 7
    uninvolved style of, 7
passive entertainment, 10
passive isolation, 12
Patrick's inspirational story, 137–139
permissive parenting style, 7
personal identity, 30
personal integrity, 29
personality traits, interaction with others and, 65–66
perspective
    benefits of, key, 80–82
    brain development and, 79
    conversation starters and, 91
    everyday lives and, 87–90
    external events and, positive and negative, 76
    gaining, eight ways to help in, 84–86

Kids Korps USA and, 79
leaders for life and, seven critical steps for developing, 166
philosophy of life and, 79
positive, 80
purpose of, 76
questionnaire, 87
sensible, 81
understanding, 82
See also compassion
perspectives of life, 164
Philanthropy Club, 164
philosophy of life, 79
physical pain (feelings of), 59–60
positive perspective, 80
possibility-thinkers, 85
priorities, high, 98
Putnam, Robert, 59

R

reaction, 63
reciprocity, spontaneous, 97
relationships
    empathetic, 64
    healthy, 61–62, 68
responsibility, 19, 21, 41

S

safety, sense of, 62
schools, safe, 16
self-absorbed, 8, 12
self-assurance, 21
self-confidence, 118
self-esteem, higher, 40–41
self-identity, 27
Selye, Hans, 18
sensible perspective, 81
Sharon's inspirational story, 148–151
shorter fuses, 57–60
    See also connection
social adjustment questionnaire, 67
social behavior, inappropriate, 64–65
social intelligence, 62
social interaction, 19
social isolation, 59–60
social mastery, 40
social rejection, 60
"soul hits" of giving, 21

spirit of interdependence, instilling, 43–44
   See also gratitude; interdependence
Spock, Benjamin, 15
strengths, 63
The Stress of Life, 18
Syme, Leonard, 18

T

Tawnya's inspirational story, 144–145
"teachable moments," 84–85
Teen Korps, 135, 147, 164–165
television
   brain and, effects on, 10–11
   programming, broad, 10
thankful life questionnaire, 106–107
"They Really, Truly Believed I Was Santa Clause" (inspirational story), 133–134
thoughtfulness, 98
Time magazine, 59
The Tipping Point, 172
Toronto Star, 171
touchstones, five essential, 25–27
   connection, 26, 55–56
   gratitude, 27, 94–96
   inspiration, 27, 114–117
   interdependence, 26, 37–39
   perspective, 26–27, 76–80

U

understanding perspective, 82
uninvolved parenting style, 7
University of Michigan, 164
University of North Carolina, 18

V

video games, 10
vision, 98
volunteer activities, types of (examples), 19, 162–163
volunteer program study, disabled and nondisabled, 18–19
volunteerism, 19, 166–167

W

Wafer, Joani, 155
Walsh, David, 115
"When I Grow Up" (inspirational story), 133
willingness, 37, 41

About the Authors

Bettie B. Youngs, PhD, EdD, is the Pulitzer Prize–nominated author of thirty-four books translated into twenty-four languages. Dr. Youngs, a former Teacher of the Year, is a university professor of graduate school education and the director of Instruction and Professional Development, Inc. Bettie has frequently appeared on *The Good Morning Show, NBC Nightly News,* CNN, and *Oprah. USA Today, The Washington Post, Time, Redbook, McCall's, U.S. News & World Report, Working Woman, Family Circle, Parents, Woman's Day,* and the NASSP (National Association of Secondary School Principals) have all recognized her work. Dr. Youngs is coauthor of the nationally acclaimed *Parents on Board* (Active Parenting Publishers), a video-based training program to help schools and parents work together to increase student achievement. She has written extensively on the dynamics of family relationships as well as the stages of development and developmental psychology for youth, families, and educators. Bettie is also coauthor along with her daughter Jennifer of the national award-winning ten-book self-help series for teens: *Taste Berries for Teens: Inspirational Short Stories and Encouragement on Life, Love, Friendship and Tough*

Issues. Dr. Youngs serves on the board for a number of organizations, including the Fuller Center for Housing. To contact: www.BettieYoungs.com.

Joanne Wolf, PhD is a former clinical psychologist and founding member of Kids Korps USA. After nearly a decade in clinical practice, Dr. Wolf turned her attention to investigating how children benefit from giving, serving, and helping others. Interested in supporting projects that strive to develop the hearts, minds, and spirits of children, Dr. Wolf serves on a number of boards and service organizations that do just that. With a penchant for adventure, she has incorporated service to others with sports and travel. Recently, she helped raise more than $600,000 to shelter and educate disadvantaged children by bicycling more than 530 miles through the mountains of New Mexico and Colorado. She also took part as a team member in supporting an athlete's bid to be the first paraplegic to summit Mount Kilimanjaro in Africa and to help spread the message, "Anything is possible." Dr. Wolf is married to David, a retired plastic surgeon. She and her husband have three grown children and take great delight in raising their fourth. To contact: www.teachingkidstocare.com.

Joani Wafer cofounded Kids Korps USA in 1994. Since then, this nonprofit organization has engaged thousands of young people, ages five through eighteen, in hands-on community service. Under her leadership as CEO, Kids Korps has grown from a grassroots to a national organization, with nearly a hundred chapters throughout the United States. *Redbook* magazine awarded Joani and her sister, Dawn, its prestigious "Mothers & Shakers" Award in honor of their "significant contribution toward promoting peace in America to ensure a safe future for children and families." California's 38th Senatorial District selected Joani Woman of the

Year. And the California State Assembly and the California Office of the Governor recognized her in regard to her work and dedication to youth volunteerism. Prior to Kids Korps, Joani spent eighteen years running a successful jewelry business. She gained her nonprofit experience volunteering for eight years with the Make-A-Wish Foundation. Joani and her husband, Chuck, have six children and two grandchildren. To contact: www.kidskorps.org.

Dawn Lehman, PhD, a cultural anthropologist and cofounder of Kids Korps USA, has developed Kids Korps programs for Boys and Girls Clubs, religious institutions, and schools in North Carolina, Michigan, and Illinois; and established College Korps, Kids Korps' volunteer mentor program for college students. She has conducted research and written professional articles on youth volunteers with disabilities. In 1999, *Redbook* magazine awarded Dawn and her sister, Joani Wafer, its "Mothers & Shakers" award for work that helps prevent youth violence, making America a safer place in which to live. Both Dawn and Joani have been interviewed by the news media in North Carolina, New York, and California. Currently, Dr. Lehman works as a senior researcher at Mather LifeWays, a nonprofit organization dedicated to enhancing the lives of older adults. She is designing an intergenerational program that brings older adults and Kids Korps youth together to serve the community. Dr. Lehman has been a member of award-winning teams of professionals that have addressed social issues associated with youth, the environment, public health, the arts, and aging. Dawn and her husband, Charlie, have four children and three grandchildren. To contact: www.kidskorps.org.

Hampton Roads Publishing Company

... for the evolving human spirit

BYB

bettie youngs books

HAMPTON ROADS PUBLISHING COMPANY
publishes books on a variety of subjects,
including spirituality, health, and other related topics.

For a copy of our latest trade catalog,
call toll-free, 800-766-8009,
or send your name and address to:

HAMPTON ROADS PUBLISHING COMPANY, INC.
1125 STONEY RIDGE ROAD • CHARLOTTESVILLE, VA 22902
E-mail: hrpc@hrpub.com • Internet: www.hrpub.com